ONLINE MUSIC: WILL SMALL MUSIC LABELS AND ENTREPRENEURS PROSPER IN THE INTERNET AGE

HEARING

BEFORE THE

COMMITTEE ON SMALL BUSINESS
HOUSE OF REPRESENTATIVES

ONE HUNDRED SIXTH CONGRESS

Fredonia Books
Amsterdam, The Netherlands

Online Music:
Will Small Music Labels and Entrepreneurs Prosper
in the Internet Age

by
Committee on Small Business
U.S. House of Representatives

ISBN: 1-4101-0877-5

Reprinted from the 2001 edition

Fredonia Books
Amsterdam, The Netherlands
http://www.fredoniabooks.com

COMMITTEE ON SMALL BUSINESS

JAMES M. TALENT, Missouri, *Chairman*

LARRY COMBEST, Texas
JOEL HEFLEY, Colorado
DONALD A. MANZULLO, Illinois
ROSCOE G. BARTLETT, Maryland
FRANK A. LoBIONDO, New Jersey
SUE W. KELLY, New York
STEVEN J. CHABOT, Ohio
PHIL ENGLISH, Pennsylvania
DAVID M. McINTOSH, Indiana
RICK HILL, Montana
JOSEPH R. PITTS, Pennsylvania
JOHN E. SWEENEY, New York
PATRICK J. TOOMEY, Pennsylvania
JIM DeMINT, South Carolina
EDWARD PEASE, Indiana
JOHN THUNE, South Dakota
MARY BONO, California

NYDIA M. VELAZQUEZ, New York
JUANITA MILLENDER-McDONALD,
    California
DANNY K. DAVIS, Illinois
CAROLYN McCARTHY, New York
BILL PASCRELL, New Jersey
RUBEN HINOJOSA, Texas
DONNA M. CHRISTIAN-CHRISTENSEN
    Virgin Islands
ROBERT A. BRADY, Pennsylvania
TOM UDALL, New Mexico
DENNIS MOORE, Kansas
STEPHANIE TUBBS JONES, Ohio
CHARLES A. GONZALEZ, Texas
DAVID D. PHELPS, Illinois
GRACE F. NAPOLITANO, California
BRIAN BAIRD, Washington
MARK UDALL, Colorado
SHELLEY BERKLEY, Nevada

HARRY KATRICHIS, *Chief Counsel*
MICHAEL DAY, *Minority Staff Director*

CONTENTS

	Page
Hearing held on May 24, 2000	1

WITNESSES

Dube, Ric, Senior Editor/Analyst, Webnoize, Cambridge, MA	3
Silverman, Tom, Founder & CEO, Tommy Boy Records, New York, NY	9
Harter, Peter, Vice-President, Global Public Policy & Standards, Emusic.com, Redwood City, CA	12
Chuck D, Founder, Rapstation.com	16

APPENDIX

Opening statements:	
Talent, Hon. James	53
Bono, Hon. Mary	55
Prepared statements:	
Dube, Ric	57
Silverman, Tom	61
Harter, Peter	67
Chuck D	81
Additional Information:	
Statement of Home Recording Rights Coalition	84
Statement of the Future of Music Coalition	89

ONLINE MUSIC: WILL SMALL MUSIC LABELS AND ENTREPRENEURS PROSPER IN THE INTERNET AGE?

WEDNESDAY, MAY 24, 2000

House of Representatives,
Committee on Small Business,
Washington, DC.

The Committee met, pursuant to call, at 11:15 a.m., in Room 2360, Rayburn House Office Building, Hon. Jim Talent [chair of the Committee] presiding.

Chairman TALENT. We will go ahead and convene the hearing. I expect the Ranking Member any minute, and if she comes after I finish my opening statement we will go right to the testimony and then we can just take a convenient moment and let her make her opening statement.

Thank you for joining the Committee today for our hearing to discuss the future of on-line music distribution models and the ways new technology will affect smaller record labels and music acts.

This is the third in a series of hearings that the Committee has held regarding e-commerce issues. It is one that is certainly very timely. So much attention these days is being devoted to the controversial music-file-swapping software Napster, it is a good time to explore how issues like piracy as well privacy concerns, marketing budget and the omnipresence of the worldwide web affect the bottom line of smaller music entities.

The advent of MP3, which is essentially a file format that allows computer users to download near CD quality music and audio files, has made listening to music via the Internet a reality for many computer users. The algorithms used to encode MP3 files compress data to convert a file that would take 40 minutes to download a regular CD format, so that takes 5 minutes to download as an MP3 file. In order to attain the smaller file size, this compression destroys some audio parts that will never be reconstructed which is why MP3 cannot reach exact CD quality. That is at least as of the time this statement was drafted, which was last night. Perhaps in the meantime the technology has changed.

As more people have access to the Internet and MP3 files, there have been various concerns voiced by various parties in the music industry. Today, one of the main concerns is Napster, which gives everyone who uses the software access to all the MP3 files on one another's computers that they are willing to share. Napster's own servers compile a large, constantly updated index of all the music available from its users. Users simply type in the song title or name of the artist they are looking for, and Napster generates a list of other users who already have it. Clicking on one of the selections automatically copies the file from one user's hard drive to the other's. It makes everybody, in essence, a music store reservoir.

Many in the music industry believes programs like Napster will cause music listeners to cease purchasing musical recordings. Indeed, a recent *New York Times* article highlights the use of Napster by a college student who downloaded 800 musical recordings from the Internet. There are others, though, who believe that free access to music via the Internet is a powerful marketing tool and that this new form of distribution will help, not hurt, sales of musical recordings.

The development of this type of software also has ramifications for the movie industry. Once this file-sharing software is perfected and digital delivery via the Internet becomes quicker, computer users may be able to swap high-quality movie files in the same way, thus affecting film studios, movie theaters, and video rental chains.

In this age of Napster and other file-sharing programs like Gnutella, the question arises as to "how will record labels and musicians control the distribution of their music and will they be able to make a profit?" The Recording Industry Association of America has undertaken the long-awaited Secure Digital Music Initiative which is working to develop an open, interoperable architecture and specification for digital music security. Once completed, purchasers of SDMI-compliant music files and software will be able to play their music in SDMI-compliant portable and home players. Until then, though, there are a multiple of file formats available on the Internet, most without the copyright protection that SDMI-compliant files are projected to have.

The music industry, as well as other industries we have examined, the Internet is purported to be able to balance the inequities faced by small entities. While it is true that smaller businesses have the flexibility to adapt quickly to changes in the marketplace, the Committee is concerned about their ability to absorb losses that may incur due to piracy.

Additionally, in the wilderness of the Internet, how will small music labels to get their voices heard above the roar of the big soon-to-be-four record labels?

To answer these questions and to provide us with an excellent background on these issues, we have a distinguished panel of witnesses.

Rick Dube is a Senior Analyst and Editor with Webnoize, which focuses on the entertainment industry's relationship with the Internet. Tom Silverman, founder and CEO of Tommy Boy Records is testifying on behalf of the RIAA. Peter Harter is Vice President for Global Public Policy and Standards of Emusic.com, the Internet's leading retailer of licensed and authorized MP3 music files. And Chuck D, recording artist and founder of Rapstation.com, which features free MP3 downloads, a television station and information for aspiring artists.

I appreciate the witnesses being here and look forward to their testimony.

Mr. Dube, we will go right ahead with you, and then when Ms. Velázquez—I am informed that Ms. Velázquez just wants to put her statement into the record; and, without objection, we will do that.

[Ms. Velázquez's statement may be found in appendix.]

Chairman TALENT. So we will go right to the witnesses.

First, staff is going to give us a demonstration of how this music can be downloaded, and also we are not going to do anything illegal here. I tried, but Mr. Andrews just passed the bar exam, and he doesn't want to lose his license. So we will go ahead and give a demonstration. And, Dwayne, why don't you explain what you are doing so the Committee members understand.

Mr. ANDREWS. Thank you, Mr. Chairman.

What I am going to do today is essentially for the Committee just to demonstrate how we can download musical files in two different formats, one being the MP3 format and the other being in the streaming audio using real player which can be downloaded from the real player website real.com. Today we are going to use the EMusic.com website, surprise, surprise, and go into the classical musical section since my tastes are a little different from the Committee member's taste as far as music is concerned.

The first thing I wanted to demonstrate is how quickly it would take to download an MP3 file onto the hard drive on this laptop computer here at the desk. I click onto the sample track MP3 file, and it starts downloading the file. This is about a 30-second file, I believe; and within seconds the file will be complete onto our hard drive and I can play it right now.

Also, this is through our regular computer speakers. These are speakers that are usually hooked up to the computers in our offices. So this 30-second snippet took about 5 seconds to download and is permanently on our hard drive until we decide to erase it.

Chairman TALENT. The technology is available to play this through higher quality speaker systems; is that right?

Mr. ANDREWS. Since it is an MP3 file I can download this onto either a portable MP3 player, Walkman-type device or even home MP3 players.

Also, I can download the same song using Real Player which is a streaming audio file which it won't be captured onto our hard drive. It is sort of just like a radio transmission. It goes through the computer and it is lost again until I click on that site again.

This, in essence, is just how easy it is to obtain music via the Internet.

Chairman TALENT. All right. Thank you, Dwayne.

Mr. ANDREWS. Thank you, Mr. Chairman.

Chairman TALENT. Now we will go to our first witness, Mr. Rick Dube, who is the Senior Editor and Analyst for Webnoize of Cambridge, Massachusetts, sir, with your statement.

STATEMENT OF RIC DUBE, SENIOR EDITOR/ANALYST, WEBNOIZE, CAMBRIDGE, MA

Mr. DUBE. Mr. Chairman and Members of the Committee, on behalf of Webnoize thank you for inviting me to testify today at this very important hearing regarding the future of music on the Internet and small businesses.

I am Rick Dube, an analyst with Webnoize and interim editor of the company's news publications. I have been on the Internet since 1991, an Internet industry professional since 1994, and I have always been a music fan and consumer, heavy-duty consumer. Ask my wife, ask my mother, I am troubled with a wallet.

Webnoize provides news coverage and analysis of the entertainment industry's relationship with the Internet, new media, cross markets and emerging technologies. Our news reports reach 75,000 industry leaders in music, film, broadcasting, technology, telecommunications, consumer electronics, media and business.

We started Webnoize with what at the time was a bold premise, that the Internet represents the single most significant outcome of the post-industrial revolution but does not represent a revolution in and of itself—it is an evolution. Evolution is bigger. The Internet represents change and progress and opportunity. Revolution is just one possibility.

Our news is published all day, every day from our offices in Cambridge, Mass. Each year in Los Angeles we host the largest, most successful annual conference showcasing and discussing how new technologies affect the entertainment industry.

We have always covered small businesses, because that is where the action is and because the Internet presents as much opportunity for them to flourish as it does massive conglomerates. The problem for both is that taking advantage of the Internet to evolve a business model requires understanding outside of the core competencies of many existing companies.

A member of the Committee asked me yesterday whether large on-line retailers like Amazon.com were hurting privately-owned music retailers. The answer is not yet. Internet sales of music are actually not all that impressive. About 1 percent of all CDs are sold on-line. That is about the same in 1999 as in 1998.

Now it is true that traditional record stores have lost about 20 percent of their market share over the last 10 years, but most of that ground has been lost to electronic superstores and department stores that sell CDs as a loss leader. If anything is hurting mom and pop record stores, it is the growth of superstores and large music chains in the real world, not the virtual world.

But I did say not yet. The Internet will affect small retailers in the long run but not because Amazon.com sells CDs. It is because the Internet is so much more interesting than a convenient place to sell CDs.

At Webnoize we have an internal slogan, one of many. We say that "the web is passe." the worldwide web is just one manifestation of the Internet. The Internet is an information network that can add functionality to any electronic device. There is a microwave oven in development by Samsung, a refrigerator by Frigidaire and wireless telephones all over Europe and Asia, all of which offer Internet connectivity.

I don't know now how much demand there is for a microwave that downloads——

Chairman TALENT. I was going to say, what could a refrigerator do on the Internet?

Mr. DUBE. Well, you would run out of the milk and you'd blip it, you could wand it in, and the next time your groceries are delivered you don't have to make a list, you don't have to go out shopping, but you can also stream music through it and leave messages for people in the house.

Chairman TALENT. Music to drink milk by or something like.

Mr. DUBE. Yeah. On the microwave, you blip the food in, and it cooks it automatically. It downloads the instructions from the Internet. I don't know if there is any demand for that.

The point is that the Internet is not just one way to use a personal computer. Thus, using the Internet to grow a business is not about putting up a dot.com site. So let me give some examples.

Traditional music retailers, traditional stores, brick-and-mortar stores like Virgin Megastores, HMV and the Trans World chains are planning ways to bring the Internet into their stores to provide more comprehensive services and create more foot traffic. One example, imagine stepping up to a kiosk in a record store, browsing through a list of the top 40 hits of the day, selecting 12 of your favorites and having a CD of them created for you while you wait. Or maybe some record that came out 30 years ago that only you cared about, you lost your copy 25 years ago and haven't seen it since. With digital Internet connections and CD burners and laser printing, nothing ever needs to be out of stock or out of print.

Another example, this is my MP3 player. I try not to go anywhere without it. This particular one was manufactured by Diamond multimedia. It weighs a couple of ounces and holds about 2 hours of digital music. I am looking forward to a day when, say I am stuck in an airport, I can pop this device in a slot in a kiosk and load it with a couple of hours of music, an hour of songs that I asked for specifically, maybe an hour of things I haven't heard of but the computer knows it is something I will probably like, and maybe that kiosk is branded by a popular record store chain, maybe it is a Tower Records kiosk, because a couple of square feet of space on the airport floor is a lot cheaper than leasing space for a whole store.

What this does, it takes the retail experience outside of stores. We are quite a ways off from that now. It is unlikely the small independent retailer would bother to participate in that sort of market opportunity, but there may be other ways for them to participate. The real opportunity for small retailers is to extend what has always been their core competency, serving consumer niches.

We already know that this is working. If you look at a survey by the National Association of Recording Merchants, Internet retail represents about 1 percent of chain store sales, but they represent about 3 percent of sales at independent stores. Indie stores have more quickly found a way to connect with their niche and serve them.

The natural course of any market is to limit the number of sellers, but that never lasts long because consumers grow frustrated when generalized services fail to meet their individual needs, and then small businesses come in and fill the gap.

Small record labels serve the same function. They release the music that the major record companies don't. It is music that plays to a significantly smaller audience but generally one that cares more about the music.

And the Internet has been a great place for independent music. Websites let small labels market their acts to audiences in ways that TV and radio could never allow. Any band that wants to promote itself on line can upload music and pictures to MP3.com or Riffage, GarageBand.com, or the Internet Underground Music Archive. MP3.com offers music by 67,000 artists, one or two of which actually make a living from the CDs they sell on the site.

The independent labels have led the charge to experiment with downloadable music. Giving away downloadable songs can be a great way to expose music that will not get air play on the radio or on MTV. By doing that, indie labels are leading a very provocative experiment, finding out whether giving away music online affects sales and, if so, in what direction.

You have probably heard about Napster. Napster has been called by music executives the most insidious development on the Internet. Whether or not it is that, it is certainly one of the most ingenious.

Napster is not a website per se but a software application that lets users swap most MP3 files back and forth. Most of the files available using Napster are illegally reproduced copies of copyright-protected music. Millions of songs are available, all for free.

Napster is most popular with college students because they have high bandwidth Internet connections that let them download music real fast. A Webnoize survey found that over 70——

Chairman TALENT. Let me just interrupt you for a minute. We explained in my opening statement what Napster was. I think it is real important that the Committee understand how it works, and would you just take a minute and explain it? When I was preparing for this hearing, I had no prior knowledge. I was a kind of a blank slate. So I don't think I am showing any disrespect to my colleagues when I say to you that don't assume a level of knowledge about Napster here. Okay? So explain how it works please.

Mr. DUBE. I might borrow a quote from them. They don't necessarily explain it in the clearest way possible—because I think—well, you know, they are in legal trouble.

What Napster lets you do is search each other's libraries of MP3 files. I have a folder on my hard drive that has a hundred MP3 files in it. Maybe one of you does as well. We both log into the Napster server, and then I can see the MP3 files on your hard drive, and you can see the names of the ones on mine. And if I want any of the ones that you have, I click on them, and it creates a direct connection between you and me through which the file transfers.

The file doesn't pass through Napster's server. Napster serves just as the conduit for us to search each other's libraries and then, when we find something we want, we click and order it, and it passes through some other chain on the Internet to get to us, to get to you or to get to me.

Mrs. BONO. Mr. Chairman, may I ask a quick, relevant question, please?

Chairman TALENT. Sure, go ahead.

Mrs. BONO. Can you please explain to me where you get the first file that you put up on Napster?

Mr. DUBE. Sure. Perfectly legal to create MP3 files from the CDs that you own for your own personal use. It is covered by various copyright law. You cannot transfer those files to somebody else for their personal use. That is an act of music piracy. Readily available software available for free anywhere that pulls the track off of the CD and then compresses it into an MP3 file. When it comes off the CD, it is like a huge, huge file; and then a compressor turns it into an MP3 file, which is about a megabyte a minute.

Mrs. BONO. Would you please explain to me the copyright infringement, let us hypothetically say——

Chairman TALENT. If the gentlelady will suspend, let us take a minute, and if you have questions, let us ask Mr. Dube the questions so we understand. Because I don't think, if we don't understand how Napster works, a lot of the rest of the testimony won't be as meaningful to you. So if anybody has a follow-up on Ms. Bono's questions, fine. And please go ahead.

Mrs. BONO. Thank you, Mr. Chairman.

Once again, so you are taking—I don't know what you listen to. Let us say it is the Eagles, Hotel California, for example. You turn that into an MP3 file, put it up on your server. It is there for anybody to come exchange with you. Can you explain to me where there is a copyright infringement at some point, correct?

Chairman TALENT. Or you might be listening to, say, a Diamond Rio song?

Mrs. BONO. Okay. Diamond Rio.

Mr. DUBE. It is a copyright infringement as soon as you traffic the file, if you are not using it for personal use. The equivalent of making a cassette of an album you want so that you can listen to it in the car, creating an MP3 file is covered by the same end of copyright law, but as soon as you transfer that file to someone else, that is an act of music piracy.

Mrs. BONO. Thank you.

Mr. DUBE. Is that a sufficient explanation?

Chairman TALENT. Does anybody else have a question on Napster?

Ms. MILLENDER-MCDONALD. Mr. Chairman, thank you very much. I did want to—and I am kind of piggybacking my colleague Mrs. Bono's question as to the copyright issue. It just appeared to have been perhaps infringement on privacy, but the privacy laws—I suppose I would like your further explanation of that.

Mr. DUBE. Privacy infringement because people can see on my hard drive?

Ms. MILLENDER-MCDONALD. Yeah. But I think you kind of explain because you say once you have seen what you want from the other party then it goes through another channel and it does not——

Mr. DUBE. It is a voluntary process. Nobody could see any files on anybody else's hard drive if that person themself wasn't logged into Napster as well at the same time.

Ms. MILLENDER-MCDONALD. It is kind of like obligatory name or your name, and then if they so choose to move into your file it goes to another channel?

8

Mr. DUBE. Yeah. A file can take zillions of routes on the Internet, and so the file takes the most direct route it can from me to you. It doesn't go through Napster. It just zips straight over to you.

As far as the privacy issue goes, I think anybody logged into Napster is there voluntarily. They have clicked on some sort of agreement.

Chairman TALENT. The point is, anybody who has Napster can log into and download quickly music of anybody else who has Napster. So, in effect, you can get anything that way.

Go ahead. Thank you.

Mr. DUBE. Real quick, I have been handed a quote from an older version of their website. With Napster you can locate and download your favorite music in MP3 format, all from one convenient, easy-to-use interface. Oh, and it is 100 percent free.

So a survey of our own finds that over 70 percent of students are using Napster at least monthly. More than 19 percent said they are using it daily.

I met one young woman who said to me that she hated dorm life, she hated the food, she hated the noise. I said, why don't you move out. She said, I don't know where I would get my music.

In that same Webnoize study, 63 percent of students said they are listening to more music downloaded from the Internet than 1 year ago; and 23 percent said they are spending significantly less time listening to CDs.

The question is whether Napster is killing the music industry. It would be rash to assume that every time someone downloads an illegal music file that the recording industry has lost a sale. When music is free, people will try a lot that they wouldn't have otherwise. And while Napster may have enabled the climate for casual piracy, the music industry is growing. Total revenue is up. CD shipments are up. However, it is possible that sales and shipments would be up even higher if it weren't for all the Internet music piracy going on.

We know that Napster is most popular with young people. The market share for music accounted for by consumers between the ages of 15 and 24 has dropped considerably over the last decade. One reason for this, music competes with games, movies, television and the Internet itself for disposable income, and there is a lot more media out there than ever before. This creates more volume, takes things away from other things, and as a result the music market has dropped for young people.

But they love Napster. We asked college students who use it whether they would be willing to pay $15 per month to use it, and more than 58 percent said that they would. It hints that it might be time for the recording industry to consider the possibility of letting people pay for music not just by the song or by the album but by the month.

Napster touts the size of its user base as its strength. They call it the Napster community, that the software enables the sense of community. They have 10 million users, and I don't know if any of them care a bit about the Napster community. I think they like Napster because that is where the content is. Record companies have released very little of their music on the Internet. Our economy operates on a supply-and-demand dynamic, and when supply fails to come through demand creates its own supply. It is sort of a perverse version of the notion that small businesses fill the niche gaps left behind when there are too few sellers.

New revenue models for music like digital distribution, subscription access, personalized radio, pay-per-view webcasts are all possible, and for now there is nothing stopping independent labels or private retailers from getting in on them, exploring them, looking for ways to improve the value of on-line music experience and the off-line music experience.

And it won't be long before the most enterprising businesses on the Internet are run by the artists themselves. It is going on now. The Internet enables music distribution and programming that fans will pay for. Artists that already have a following will leave the established music label systems and strike out on their own.

Webnoize values companies like Napster because they have great ideas and they put them in action. Just as major labels watch to see which independent artists have wide commercial potential, they are also watching smart young companies to see which ideas to co-opt.

Thank you for the opportunity to testify. I would be happy to answer any questions that you have.

Chairman TALENT. Thank you, Ric. We will have further questions after all the witnesses have testified, and thank you for your very informative testimony.

[Mr. Dube's statement may be found in appendix.]

Chairman TALENT. Our next witness is Mr. Tom Silverman, who is the founder and CEO of Tommy Boy Records of New York, New York. Mr. Silverman.

STATEMENT OF TOM SILVERMAN, FOUNDER & CEO, TOMMY BOY RECORDS, NEW YORK, NY

Mr. SILVERMAN. Thank you. I passed around—I guess everybody has got a copy of my testimony, but I am not going to read my testimony. I am going to go freestyle.

Chairman TALENT. That is always preferable. Please do.

Mr. SILVERMAN. I want to tell you a little bit about myself. About 20 years ago, I got a loan of $5,000 from my parents, and I started Tommy Boy music in my bedroom in an apartment in New York City. I was the only employee at the time, and I didn't know what was going to happen, but we just had a few good breaks, and we are still in business today, and we have about 140 employees now and an office in London.

Chairman TALENT. Would you move the mike a little closer?

Mr. SILVERMAN. Yeah. So our company has grown to be one of the largest, if not the largest, independently distributed label in America. And at various times we have been involved with major labels as well, so I have a pretty good perspective of both.

We present artists like Everlast, De La Soul, Capone and Noreaga. We had artists like Digital Underground, House of Pain, Queen Latifah, RuPaul, Naughty by Nature, Africa Bambaata, Force MD and many, many others. We are in the music business in many genres, not just rap music but also dance music, gospel music now, and rock music, as well as we are preeminent in the compilation business.

I would like to talk a little bit about what a record company does. This is what all record companies do—independent labels, small labels and large labels, the majors. Really, record companies find music that they think will have a demand with consumers, and they contract the services of the artist. Then they help the artist to make the record, in most cases. Then they market the record.

So they put up all the money to do this and to market the record; and the marketing would include everything from radio promotion to making videos, to giving tour support, to promoting the record in clubs and other venues, to advertising, many, many different ways to get exposure. And now we have added another weapon to the arsenal of promotion, which is the Internet as another medium to allow people to find out about the music.

All of this stuff is very expensive, and whether it is an independent label or a major label, a very small proportion of the records that we sign or release actually make a profit for us. So the ones that do make a profit end up having to pay for all the ones that don't. It is a real crapshoot.

But the difference between an independent label and a major label, Ric started to discuss a little bit, because we have to be niche finders. We have to find music. Especially the smaller labels—we have to get into the music that the majors aren't in because they will crush us because they take all the slots and we won't get any exposure.

So when I started in 1981, for example, rap music was a new thing. There were maybe only like 20 rap groups in the world. So we had an idea to put out rap records, and there wasn't that much competition, and no major labels were in it. So we were able to build our company with the growth of rap as a musical genre. We were faster, and we were more creative than the majors, and we weren't afraid of doing something unknown.

The other thing that makes independent labels—you know, this is probably true of all small businesses—is that we are under-capitalized, and we are working without a net. If we make too many mistakes, we are out of business. There is nobody who is going to bail us out. Forget about getting a loan, we don't get loans. My loan was $5,000 from my dad. He got paid back in a year because I got a lucky break, and I had a small hit record that broke in New York within the first year. Otherwise, he wouldn't have gotten his money back. But that is the nature of an independent label, and it is really true today.

I have served on the board of the Association for Independent Music for 13 years. I have been on the board of NARM, which is the National Association of Record Merchandise. I am currently also on the board of the RIAA as an independent label member.

I would like to mention a few facts about the music industry that are very relevant and very few people know. In 1999 in America there were 38,856 albums released; 31,933 of those albums came from the independent labels. So the vast majority of the releases came from the independent label community.

In that same year, of the records released in that year, in the independent sector, only 257 titles that were released out of that 31,933 that they released sold over 25,000 units. And I think it is pretty safe to say that if you didn't sell 25,000 units probably you didn't make money on that record because it costs so much money to make and market music. And, for example, probably 20,000 releases by the independents didn't even sell 1,000 units; and, in fact, industry-wide only 1.1 percent of all the releases sell over 100,000 units. That includes the majors and the indies. So these are factors to keep in mind.

When you hear about the Backstreet Boys doing 2.4 million or N'Sync doing 2.4 million units the first week, that is one release. That may be 10 percent of all the record sales in that release week. It is very top heavy, just the way it is with retail. In retail, the top 10 accounts are 70 percent of all record sales. So it is true with artists as well.

So you have this dichotomy between the massive artists that sell all the records and the tens of thousands of releases that sell almost nothing to core niche markets, and the independents dominate that market. Every now and then one of those records breaks through and becomes really big, and the majors go out and try and snatch it up, keeping the independents at around 16 percent of the market share for overall sales. They do only 16 percent—between 15 and 18 percent of the market share with, you know, with 80 percent or 85 percent of all of the releases that come out. So that is a fact.

And you gave the fact that 67,000 artists have their music online. And it is pretty safe to say that 66,999 of those are artists that probably don't even have a record out that sold a hundred units and that nobody's really interested in owning. I may be wrong about that, but somebody would have to correct me if I am.

I really believe the technology will help drive the future of our business for the independent labels and for the major labels. We can't be afraid of it, but technology is really just a conduit for our content. It is the messenger. It is not the message.

I was really disturbed when I was at my mother's house for Mother's Day, and my cousin was there, and he was listening to a CD in the car, and he was kind of holding it secretively. And he had made this CD himself in his computer on his own CD burner. He is 11 years old, and he had downloaded from Napster one of my songs off of the Internet. Eleven years old. We are not talking college students here.

A CD burner which is how you can make your own CD. What you described, yes, you can download it onto this or you can burn your own CD and make an infinite number of copies of those CDs and sell them or give them away to whoever you want. So the fact that he was able to do that isn't what disturbed me—well, I guess it did disturb me that he could figure it out and he was into it so fast. I thought it would take a while before it was going to get down to the 11 year-olds, but it didn't really take that long.

The other thing that really bothers me is I had a meeting with my biggest artist who just sold three million albums on his last release and has a new single out, won a Grammy with Santana for a song called, *Put Your Lights On,* which is coming out this week as a single on another label. He brought his new album, which will come out in the fall, and he played it for us, but he wouldn't leave the DAT, the tape of the music with us because he was afraid of it showing up on Napster and—or anywhere on the Internet before the release so that everybody would have it. Because he says routinely you can get records a month before they are even out free online.

It is bad enough you are losing the sales, but you are also losing the elements of surprise that, okay, Tuesday it is in the store, everybody gets excited. Well, I have had the record for a month already; I just downloaded it. That is another issue.

All of my biggest artists now—this is a new thing—refuse to give me copies of their work in progress. They will not let anyone in the record company, not even their A&R person, the person who makes the record with them, hold any of the music because they are so afraid of this music leaking out and being on there.

De La Soul gave me a copy of their CD, and the copy has three times over every single song on their new album, property of Tom Silverman, to make sure that if it gets out he knows where it came from. So I can't even listen to the music without this guy's voice all over it. The same thing with Capone and Noreaga. They will not leave a copy in our office. They refuse to do that.

The combination of Napster and the piracy that is going on in the street which can also be aided and abetted by the Internet has made it really difficult for us to actually set up and market these records because we can't hear them and live with them. They have to play them and then bring them back. So I feel for them, but it is affecting us in a different way.

So, you know, that is where we are at right now. Those are some issues that we are dealing with. And I am open to questions.

Chairman TALENT. Thank you. I am sure there will be a lot of questions for you later, Mr. Silverman.

[Mr. Silverman's statement may be found in appendix.]

Chairman TALENT. Our next witness is Peter Harter, who is the Vice President of Global Public Policy and Standards of EMusic.com, Redwood City, California. Peter.

STATEMENT OF PETER HARTER, VICE PRESIDENT, GLOBAL PUBLIC POLICY & STANDARDS, EMUSIC.COM, REDWOOD CITY, CALIFORNIA

Mr. HARTER. Thank you, Mr. Chairman and members of the Committee. It is a pleasure to be here this morning.

First, a little bit of history about EMusic as a small business. And I am going to describe EMusic and some of the issues that have been raised so far this morning from my own personal point of view as well.

I have been on the Internet since 1986, and I have used all these file-sharing technologies to exchange information, to access information. Frankly, in college in the 1980s, I used file-sharing technology to access publications from computer servers at universities all over the world to help me with my work on my papers I had to write for class. So file-sharing technology is not a bad thing. It is just how people use it may be controversial or illegal.

But, first, about EMusic, about 2½ years old, originally started as a company called GoodNoise, but changed the name, when we bought another company, to EMusic. It was started by two people, Gene Hoffman, who is our President and CEO; and Bob Kohn, who is our Chairman.

Gene is one of those many young executives. He is now 24 years old. When he started the company, he was 22; and EMusic is his third company. His first company called PridNet he started in college, and within a year he sold it to a another company called Pretty Good Privacy, moved out of North Carolina to California, worked for Pretty Good Privacy, and PGP, Pretty Good Privacy, was sold to network associates. So after that Gene and Bob, who met at PGP, decided to start a company in the on-line music area. This MP3 craze was very, very popular back in 1997 and 1998.

Bob Kohn, he is a lawyer by training. He is from New York originally, and his family grew up in L.A. His father worked for Warner/Chappell Music Publishing for 25 years, and Bob was an entertainment lawyer working for a firm in L.A. That firm did work for Liza Minnelli and Frank Sinatra. Then Bob moved north out of Hollywood to Silicon Valley early on in the 1980s to work for software companies before anyone really knew or cared about software. He was general counsel for a company called Borland and fought many legal battles on copyrights and standards and really kind of shaped the industry.

But he and his father had a joint effort. They published a book on music licensing. It is literally 1,500 pages thick; and all the lawyers in the music industry, from the major labels to professors, refer to this as the foundation for understanding music licensing.

So you combine Gene, who understands technology and new trends in technology, with Bob, who understands music licensing, you have a very powerful combination for a legal business in the on-line music world where copyright law and Internet often collide and people don't understand how to apply copyright law on the Internet.

I have been with EMusic for about a year, and in the time I have been there we have grown dramatically. We are the largest retailer of music online. Not many people actually try and sell music online for a variety of reasons that have been discussed already on this panel. But we believe as a philosophy in our small business that if we make it easier, more convenient and, frankly, more fun and interesting to buy music, then people won't bother trying to hunt down some random file and download it and it turns out not to be the file you wanted in the first place. And piracy or free music, a lot of college kids go after this where they put their own music on the Internet, and there has been piracy before, and certainly the Internet is accelerating piracy.

These are important issues. So I think as a business you work hard enough and build up a loyal customer base, as we have, and have a lot of great content from nearly 700 independent labels, the small guy, you are going to make revenue.

We are actually making revenue. We are an Internet company, and we have revenue. There is a lot of talk on Wall Street about how Internet companies don't have any real revenue. We have revenue from advertising because of a lot of traffic on our site but also from the sale of music and we use the open MP3 format.

EMusic has been also a participant in something you mentioned earlier in your opening comments, Mr. Chairman, which I want to comment on briefly. There is this standards effort called SDMI. It has been going on for nearly 2 years; and, frankly, it is not going very far. I would not put your hopes on security unleashing on-line music. The train has left the station.

In this industry, you have to have a good business, great content and loyal customer base. You have to draw them in, your audience, and we have done that in a variety of ways.

We charge a very low price for music. It is only 99 cents a track or $8.99 an album, and if you happen to buy a few tracks and then come back and want to buy the whole album, we will credit back the tracks you already bought.

If your hard drive crashes—and, of course, PCs never break down these days—because you are a customer and we have your profile secure and protected—we protect your privacy, we have a privacy policy and all that, we take privacy very seriously—we have your profile, what you bought, you bought it with your credit card, and you come back and say, hey, my computer got stolen, my hard drive crashed, I can't access the music I bought, we will give it all back to you. And because we pay royalties to the rights holders, because those are actually new copies of the music, we will repay the royalties again to the rights holders.

So everybody wins. And because there is no physical goods, we download the music, all those costs of physical distribution and marketing, they are removed from the business model. So we can charge lower prices to consumers and have higher profit margins to us and the content owners, the artists and independent labels.

So it is a fantastic business model. It has grown rapidly. We have over 100,000 tracks for sale on our site and nearly 700 independent record labels with us, and it is just going wonderfully. We have about 200 employees, mostly in Redwood City, in Silicon Valley, California. We have a large number of employees in Chicago.

We have a company called RollingStone.com which we bought last year, and that provides some editorial content about music. RollingStone is a wonderful brand.

We bought a company called IUMA, the Independent Underground Music Archive, that helps artists who are not commercial become commercial. And, frankly, with our relationships with independent labels, if you are not a commercial artist but you want to meet the independent labels which is, as Tom pointed out, actually how you get a record released, we have that whole food chain lined up pretty logically.

And we have offices in Los Angeles, of course; New York, of course; people in Nashville and Austin, because that is where music comes from; and we are looking at overseas expansion eventually as we grow.

But we are a small business, started out of Gene's living room in his house, and it is just going really well.

As for Napster and piracy, we have been watching the lawsuit for some time. Bob Kohn, our Chairman, has made statements in the press about the litigation but more so as a music licensing expert.

The company is not taking an official position because it is difficult for companies to take positions on matters of litigation when they are not involved. It is something you don't want to say publicly. So I am going to be a bit guarded in my remarks.

But if you look at what is happening in the industry, people often say that the music industry is actually a $100 billion industry trapped inside a $40 billion straitjacket. It is because of the distribution. The traditional business model like the five major record labels suffocates the release of music. The independents, as Tom pointed out, release 80 to 85 percent of the content but only garner between 15 and 18 percent of the revenue. And, actually, I have figures that say they garner 25 percent of the revenue, but you get the point. There is a huge imbalance.

And surely the majors have more revenue because they have the big pop stars that are here today and gone tomorrow, like Britney Spears. She is kind of the poster child for what characterizes the major label. Now I personally don't have anything against Britney Spears, but just in the industry circle she is often held up as the example of what the majors bring to the marketplace.

The independent record labels, they bring new genres, they create new markets, they get the small artists out to the market. And the Internet completely goes around the major record labels. Now, of course, with SDMI and other tactics the majors are trying to regain control over the Net. But the train has left the station, and we have to focus on the issue of piracy. Because if the artist does not get paid, why would they create music?

EMusic pays all the royalties. It is all on the computer. So if anybody wants to come look and say, hey, I didn't get paid; why are you holding my money back from me? We will show them this is how many charts got downloaded, and there is the check; it went to your bank account.

So we offer a very good way to open up the industry and its accounting practices to show that we pay the publishers and the rights holders; and we are trying to automate it, pay more frequently than once a year or once every 2 years. Pay it monthly, maybe even daily, if we can scale it fast enough.

So a lot of great things about selling music legally in open formats on Internet.

Another thing about MP3 and why it is so popular is the format is easy to use. Sure, the sound quality can be better, but, frankly, if you are going to download music into a little portable device—not the same device that my colleague has—you are running down the street, there are buses going by, you are not going to care about having 100 percent quality music. It is good enough, it is fast, it is fun, it is convenient.

Chairman TALENT. That is a question I did want to clarify and I almost asked you, Ric, because I was told that the quality is less than CD quality but it is good enough for practical purposes. Is that a consensus here?

Mr. HARTER. I don't think it is that black and white. We encode our music files in MP3 at the highest quality, it is something called 120 fitness, and there is no point going into what that means.

The fact is, when you take a music file which is a very large file and compress it so you can store it and transmit it conveniently, what is happening is you are taking out the ones and zeroes—you are taking out the sounds the human ear cannot hear, and that may diminish the higher end music that—classical music has all these nuances, and some genres may suffer, but I think technology is changing so rapidly and the encoders are getting better, it is getting near CD quality, if not there already, and we encode it in the highest quality encoders right now. So our sound quality is very, very good at EMusic.

In closing, Mr. Chairman, I brought these props along.

Elvis Costello is one of our artists. All his music, except for some recent stuff, is on our site. This is an album he put out in 1977, Elvis Costello's *My Aim is True*; and I have got this thing in here. I don't want to damage it. My friend gave it to me.

Remember these? I used to have 1,000 of these things. When I moved from Pennsylvania to California, I couldn't lug all these things across the country, and that was 5, 6 years ago, so I gave them away or sold them. I have a few as mementos. I never play them anymore.

But we have gone from round plastic—and, of course, a CD is round plastic. I won't bother showing that. People know what a CD is.

Now, in these devices or on your computer like Dwayne's computer up there, you have silicon. It is square, square music. This is a portable memory device. It is a chip that contains music. So as if you were to take an album and make copies of the songs you like on to your audio cassettes for personal, fair use, of course and you were to play the cassette in your Walkman to go running—we have all done that—or just to play the songs you want, this is the digital progression of that.

People make their own compilations. The thing about silicon it puts the power into the hand of the artists and the consumers. The major record labels, when vinyl was king, they controlled, but control is gone from the vinyl in the majors, and control is shifting to the artists and consumers and to silicon. It is going from southern California, of Hollywood, to northern California, Silicon Valley.

Thank you.

Chairman TALENT. Thank you, Peter.

[Mr. Harter's statement may be found in appendix.]

Chairman TALENT. Our final witness is one of the most powerful advocates for cutting-edge use of the Internet to market music. He is Chuck D, founder of Rapstation.com.

Chuck, thank you for your patience; and please proceed.

STATEMENT OF CHUCK D, FOUNDER, RAPSTATION.COM

CHUCK D. I thank you, Mr. Talent, and it is coincident because I have been regarded as talent in the industry, it has taken advantage of talent.

Chairman TALENT. I wish I were as highly regarded in my line of work. Go ahead.

CHUCK D. I would also ask that these doors be closed, because, you know, that is kind of distracting, and beepers and cellies be turned off, please.

First of all——

Chairman TALENT. If the members of Congress wish to come in, I have to let them in, though.

Ms. MILLENDER-MCDONALD. Do we have to?

CHUCK D. I feel like Reggie Miller. I have got this shot clock in front of me.

But, first of all, I would like to say I admire the comments and facts and figures and respect everything that Mr. Dube and Mr. Harter has said in their business models, so I am not going to repeat many of the same things that they said; and in all due respect to Tommy Silverman, who I have worked with before, great guy, and he also has a fantastic business model as an independent record company, all due respect; but the major corporations have caused the conditions that made it difficult for independent companies and artistry to compete in the game of music.

We at Rapstation.com, and I have been involved in downloadable distribution for about 5 years as a saving grace for my artistry, have used downloadable digital distribution to microfocus upon a niche of rap music that I have been involved with. It has helped build a world community through communication, cultural exchange, in 40 countries I deal with on a regular—and I take advantage of rap's worldwide experience, and I just think the corporate imbalances of the images making rap music and hip hop, like jail, gun ganging, drug culture is sort of like balanced out with everybody participating into the reflecting imagery.

At Rapstation.com I also engage with thousands of artists to equally market their music without complaint because they control and own their own destiny. So I choose artistry over industry any day of the week.

Also, we also have to realize technology whips technology's ass every time. The 20th century tree that was so fruitful, you might not be able to pick from so easily. Napster or downloadable distribution, like we would call it, file sharing, is leading one million MP3 march. It trades music like baseball cards, and digital distribution and file sharing is like those asteroids that wiped out all the dinosaurs. And in this case the dinosaurs are the big four, Sony, BMG, Time Warner and Universal.

Now these companies, which will soon probably be three any week now, have always prided itself in the excitement of the music industry and the fans. Well, Napster and downloadable distribution is the biggest excitement since disco, rap and the Beatles. It is like new radio. And it is not just free music, but it is a watchdog method for one site industrial rip-off. The chickens have finally come home to roost.

I think if people look at the artificial price hiking of CDs, something they made for as little as 80 cents and then charged the consumers, in cahoots with retail, for as high as $17, that has never been explained to the public up until recently. They have taken advantage of the artist and the public, squeezing out the small entrepreneur with a lawyer-accountant mentality, and now the industry is now begging government for this illusion for their inconvenience.

I think the Federal Trade Commission, you know, also found out the record companies were actually hiking their prices on the public; and they said, okay, how do you feel as an artist?

First of all, I think the system had to be eradicated for everybody to participate and start from scratch. I mean, for the first time now you have who was deemed as the consumer in the audience, now they are participating in the music business. And how do we get paid? Well, technology will be there again, but the select process and the dominance will be eradicated, and now things will truly be shared. A business model will come up out of this in the new century. It won't destroy the old companies, but it will reconfigure their ways.

Piracy, well, the talk of the label 's bottom line is always the case, and that is why they are screaming. To protect artists, that is some BS.

You know, they come up with these promo copies and they press up 5,000 or 10,000 and, you know, in many of the cases they go to waste. And the downloadable distribution, you have something that is called on demand, and I know that there is an artist graveyard out there of artists, especially black artists, back since Bessie Smith in 1923, that have much more complaints than downloadable distribution. Their complaints happen to be with the one-sided contracts.

I have signed a contract that said worldwide rights, and they couldn't sell the records in Africa, South America or Asia. So why am I signing something that says worldwide rights?

Then they say, well, the world and the universe. So that means if I get to Venus, they got the right to sell my records? So they want to control cyberspace, too, without knowing what it is.

I would bet, because of the corporate quagmire, more than 50 percent of all artistry is just stuck on shelves or never comes out in the public anyway. So I think it is very imperative for artists to adapt to the technology, to try to avoid this one-sided monopoly, because I do think it is collusion, for companies now have to share the marketplace; and I look forward to one million artists and one million labels all on the Internet.

Now, RIAA, they only answer to people, you know, who are usually former lawyers and accountants who have assumed executive jobs, taking in as high as eight-figure salaries. I have never seen eight figures, but to look at a company's president who is using stockholders' money and pulling in $18 million for a year, when he gets fired, as an artist I have got a beef. So, you know, if it ain't about the artist, the industry damn sure ain't caring about the fans either, because why would they charge them $17 for something that they make for 79 cents? So I think this organizes and creates a new infrastructure.

New templates will be created. Yes, 95 percent of all music will be free, but it has always been 5 percent that have driven it. And now it is a global entertainment business. And I think the biggest beef, just like Mr. Harter said, is that now the entertainment business—and we are not just talking records companies, we are talking movie industry and television—the entertainment business is morphing into the entertain net business. And now you have technology companies that will actually push the button, as opposed to these ex-lawyers and accountants that just happen to push pencils and somehow fall into a 9 million a year salary there. I still don't know what they got paid for.

So will I think it will hurt actual sales? Nope. They said the same thing back in 1967 with FM radio. They said the same thing with the advent of the cassette recorder. The same beefs popped up. People can tape, but they will still go to Blockbuster. If they can get HBO and Cinemax and Showtime and they can tape on their VCR, what makes them go to Blockbuster? Blockbuster depends on them people bringing back their videos 8 days late. That is how they make their money.

So these companies will still be around. I think the laziness of the American public will also keep the entertainment or the entertain net business at an all-time high. And this new digital distribution will be exposure, and now, truly, we have global exposure.

So, I mean, I am here testifying in the United States of America in front of Congress, but the Island of Dominica has nothing to do with this government and, therefore, they will get the music, too, and then all of a sudden you will have Asia, Africa and South America be able to get the music.

So I think it is imperative now that the artists also understand that they can go to these places and become business people of their own or set up their own business teams instead of being locked outside the door because they don't happen to be in the offices of New York, L.A. or Nashville. So now the hands are all in the pot together. There is a million hands in the pot, and that is why you hear a lot of screaming.

I am not screaming. I had ties with Universal, Universal, Edgar B and the Universal Crew. And I had a lawyer tell me, well, Chuck, you sold millions of records here, but you will never see a dime because you owe us. And I said, like hell I do.

So you think I am caring about them? No. I am doing better in the digital system selling 10 copies, even if 100 people or 1,000 or 1,000,000 people get my music for free. If I know 1,000 that is coming my way, I will deal with that as opposed to somebody being shady.

Ms. MILLENDER-MCDONALD. Mr. Chairman.

Chairman TALENT. I think the witness can continue if he wants to, as long as he would like to.

CHUCK D. I have got to go to London tomorrow. I really have nothing else to say.

Ms. MILLENDER-MCDONALD. I would like to ask Mr. Chuck D, "how do you really feel?"

CHUCK D. Well, I know that, you know, here in Congress, I know you have many a stuffy day. I am seeing C–SPAN many a day where the cameraman was like—so why not bring a little bit of the entertain net business in the House?

Chairman TALENT. We were counting on it. You delivered as always. Thank you so much.

[Chuck D's statement may be found in appendix.]

Chairman TALENT. We will go to some questions. I have a couple, and then I want to defer to members who have been so patient.

I don't think anybody referred to something that is going on in the business that again is important for background; and maybe, Ric, you can comment on this. We talked before about Napster. And for those members who came in late, Napster is a software program that millions of people have and through which you can access other people's reservoir of music. So if you want a song you can go on Napster and download it from somebody else's file without paying for it. This is at least the concern.

There is a lawsuit going on now—Ric, would you just tell us about that, please—against Napster.

Mr. DUBE. Dealing with three lawsuits right now. One from the Recording Industry Association of America for contributor copyright infringement and vicarious copyright infringement, and then two artists have sued the company as well, Metallica and Dr. Dre.

Chairman TALENT. So there is an attempt to control this—since I think most people recognize you can't control it through the consumers—to control it through the people who are selling the software.

One question I had, is any of that going to be effective? I think somebody referred to the fact that there is going to be no way to have security kind of blocks or to control the use of this anyway, even if legally Congress tried to do it or the courts tried to do it. I think, Peter, you talked about that. Maybe, Tom, you can comment, or anyone who wants to. Because all this discussion about whether we should or shouldn't do this is, in effect, moot because it is going to happen whether it is legal or illegal?

Mr. SILVERMAN. I think it is important to recognize that copyrights have value and that they are proprietary. Because if you lose that, I could go out and take the software from Napster and start Tomster tomorrow and get my $15 million from Wall Street, which is what happened like last week or this week with Napster, to finance another kind of theft operation, you know, that frees up somebody else. And then somebody will steal my thing because nothing is protected.

I mean, this country is really based, especially small businesses, on ideas, great ideas. That is all we have, because we don't have money.

When I started my company, I had an idea. When I heard Afrika Bambaata DJ and how he put this stuff together, I said, man, let's—make a record. I didn't know what I was doing. He goes, all right, why not? And that is how the company really started.

It was just an idea, and that is intellectual property. If there is no way to control it, movies, books, television, nothing creative has any value anymore. You know, software is all up for grabs, and why would anybody be creative then? It becomes a Nation of thieves, and it is almost like a riot. Let us go loot the Pathmark.

Chairman TALENT. Chuck, tell us why anyone would be creative under those?

CHUCK D. I think you have to adapt to technology, and none of those really—except for books, none of those things meant anything in the previous century. So what we are talking about, intellectual property and certain laws, existed within the paradigm I guess of the 20th century.

Now in the 21st century it would take some kind of adaptation to whatever is going to come along, and a whole new set of rules may be set up, but as we go along we will figure those things out, but it is old hat.

What happened last century, like I said, was a whole different type of tree. And now as we go into the next century, I look at it as an artist, it is almost like being an outfielder. Now it is raining on the outfield grass, but the umpire says play ball anyway. I know I can't haul tail over in the corner trying to catch a fly ball if the field is wet, so I have got to figure out how to run on that wet grass and make do with what is there.

So my whole thing is I know how to adapt. How a major super dinosaur corporation is going to adapt—I don't care about Time Warner's bottom line. I don't care about Sony, BMG or Universal's bottom line. I just don't.

To me, if I make something for $10 and $20 comes in, boom, now I can get a fish sandwich and a peach drink. But, you know, the way those cats have swindled the public on, as far as, you know, stockholders' money and how they all went in there and raided those companies and pulled all the money out and now they are crying and saying, well, they are protecting the artist, that is just a crock of BS.

They just should say, "hey, you know we want to become richer than we were in the last century; we want to get paid more for than we did in the last century. And this is why it is bothering us." Because they have made it in the industry, they created the auspices of creating artists that are disposable every year around and throwing them out so they won't renegotiate. So they say the artists never renegotiate, but the executive salaries go up.

And I say that Tommy is an exception to the rule because he is an independent owner of a company. Yes, he has dealings with those guys, but he is not one of those guys. You don't see one of those guys here.

You know, I would like to see Edgar Bronfman, Jr., here or a head from Time Warner or a head from Sony or a head from BMG, and I would torch them. But I have got respect for Tom because I know he is dealing with elements that have got to keep him afloat because he has been torched by the same climate that these guys have concocted.

Chairman TALENT. I wish we had them here. Boy, it would be fun.

And you will just respond as you want, but also please include the answer to this. My interpretation is that what is happening here is the technology may make the middleman unnecessary, and if that is the case, as difficult as that is for the middleman or the middleperson, isn't that just something that a lot of mom and pop grocery stores aren't in business anymore because of Wal-Mart either?

Mr. DUBE. Mr. Talent, copyright laws are incredibly important, but it would be tragic if an industry used copyright law to ignore the demand of the public. You have supply and demand. It is called demand. It is not, pretty please, can we have downloadable music? They are saying, by any means necessary, this is what we want.

Now the way things are going, it would enable record labels to sell direct to the public, but that is not their core competency. Their core competency is building artists, marketing them, production, distribution. That is what they are good at. There is a whole set of middlemen that are good at getting the music to people, helping people connect with the music that they have never heard of that they will love, and so it is an evolution that everybody has to go through. It is no different from a century ago, horse raisers going out of business unless they wanted to turn their factories into car shops.

Chairman TALENT. I promise you, Tom, if you want to comment, go ahead.

Mr. SILVERMAN. There is two ways to look at it. There is the issue about artists/labels, be they big or be they small, losing revenue, you know, and that is artists and labels. So that, for example, someone yesterday called me and said, "I hear you are going to give testimony tomorrow, I want you to know about this artist called The Magnetic Field. They are a small artist, but they have a devout, college-oriented audience. Their music is a little bit left field, but they have like a triple box set, triple album box set out now that has sold 30,000 units. That is an enormous number, and they are a tiny, tiny, tiny independent label that probably does a tiny amount of business. And this guy Stephen Merritt, who is the head guy in the group, is very, very concerned because he thinks he could lose half of his business, because that is exactly who the core of the Napster world is, college kids, really." So that is one argument.

The other argument is, you know, what it costs to make a record. And if it is of interest to anybody I could break it down, because Chuck oversimplifies.

It is not 75 cents for a piece of plastic. It is not at all. I did talk about it a little bit, but, you know, it is $2 to the artist and the publishers, it is $1 for manufacturing, and it is $2 for marketing, and it is $2 for distribution, and it is $2 against the massive overheads or the small overheads of the labels, you know. And all that equals $10, and the $10 is what they sell it to the distributor or I mean the one-stops or the retailers for. And then they mark that record up from the $10 to whatever they charge, $15, $18, whatever, and that is what the retailers make.

If there is this disintermediation that you are talking about, who is going to be disintermediated? Will it be the retailer? Will it be the record company? Will it be a little of both? I don't know, and time will work that out.

I am trying to find a new way to look at the entire record business now and have a pioneer-like leadership role in changing the whole model between artists and labels. Because Chuck is pointing out things that in the new age are more and more clear that they don't work.

We have a model that has a percentage in there for breakage of when records were 78s, and they used to break all the time. It is still in the contract. He is totally right about that stuff, and I am not down with that. It is just what the tradition was, so that is what we do.

But I think now we are at a crossroads. It is a time to re-examine our relationship with an artist. Because an artist will always need a partner to finance their career, especially at the beginning in terms of how are they going to get exposure. Because it is all about mass impressions. Television, radio, movies, whatever, is mass impression, secondary college radio, college touring, press and the Internet. At some point, the Internet might be a massive impression provider like TV might be and like cable has become, but right now it is all still really radio and TV specific.

Chairman TALENT. If you are not selling the exclusive right to own that artwork because it is no longer possible to protect that exclusive right or because we choose no longer to protect it, then what are you going to be selling? What is it you can make money off of?

Mr. SILVERMAN. No one is going to be able to invest in breaking Public Enemy and no one can pay Bill Adler to publicize it.

CHUCK D. Those days are over, Tom. Them days are over.

You are going to have a million artists out there. Technology has allowed many people to have these home studios where they are making record-ready material, and there is not enough room for the major or independent companies that are your size to actually sign everybody. But they are going to actually have all their art out there, and those areas on the Internet are going—you are going to see and more and more radio stations appear on the Internet, television stations appear on the Internet in a short amount of time.

You are talking about radio station screaming. Look at an old network like CBS. They are going to be screaming because the attention span—as far as everybody going elsewhere for entertainment, nobody's going to visit CBS. I mean, they treat it like a goldfish bowl now.

What I am saying is, you are going to have a massive—and it is not just going to be national. You are going to have a massive international pot of artistry, as many as 10 million artists who made their material in their basements. And now, you know, the majors are going to try to say, well, we don't want that little kid from Ohio to actually outshine us, but we can't purchase everybody's copyrighted material. We are going to have to figure something else out.

Mr. SILVERMAN. They would just wave money in front of them like they always do.

CHUCK D. But they can't wave money in front of everybody.

Chairman TALENT. What value are you going to add to this artwork since you are not going to be able to protect the exclusive right—what are you going to offer the consumer that is going to make them go to you, the legitimate business? Even those words are going to go out. It is going to go to you instead of somebody else. How are you going to make money? I guess that is what I am asking.

Mr. HARTER. I think that is the big question. Internet business models offering high-quality sound recordings on-line at a convenient, all-one-stop-shopping site, where, you know, you go there and you don't have to hunt around for hours on end.

Napster is interesting in that its library of music is only as big as the number of people who are logged on at the time that you are on. So you can be on Napster one day and you find the track you want, but, hey, I have got to run out and do something and come back, you can't find it again. That is not the same easy, fun experience that consumers enjoy by going to a commercial retailer where the music is there, its quality is not a fraudulent copy.

Artists who are not commercially an optimal label, their music tracks are on the Net with famous names of the song, inducing somebody to download in the hopes they will listen to it and then go and track down that real music. So you think you are downloading the U2 song, *Where the Streets Have No Name,* and it is some thrash metal band, and that is not what you are looking for.

Mr. SILVERMAN. Or you didn't pay so you got your money's worth.

Mr. HARTER. That is a very good point, too, if you didn't buy it from a legal site.

What I will say about Napster, they are start up, they are a small business, they have made some tactical errors in their litigation in how they structured their business. I am not sure how sophisticated they are, but there are a lot of interesting relics in Silicon Valley.

There was a company in 1995 called Point Cast. Anybody remember Point Cast? The start up that was pushing content to you, as opposed to you going out and getting content. It would push content to you, and it was so popular that Murdoch was going to pay almost a half billion dollars for it, but Point Cast wanted more money. I think what happened to Point Cast, their executives left, they didn't make any revenue, and it was sold to somebody else for $10 million, and that company is in trouble now, too. So Napster could be the great new business or it could be the next Point Cast.

I think a lot of things in Silicon Valley depend upon who you hire, how sophisticated the management is, who your partners are. And if Napster is going to be a player in the on-line music area they have to have good relations with artists. And, frankly, if they are not paying out royalties to artists, besides maybe some promotion, I frankly as a businessperson don't see how they are going to provide a competitive advantage to artists.

Artists can go on-line like Chuck D right now and do their own thing, or maybe the majors will reform themselves and be more competitive, but I think Napster is going to be one of these end notes like Point Cast in the industry. There are a lot of factors at play here; and, as Tom said, let us wait for time to play things out.

Chairman TALENT. Chuck, you want to make a comment? And when you do—because I think it is a fair point Tom made. You are so big in the business that you can do a different business model and you are going to still do okay and you may do better. What about the new artist trying to get a toehold, needs to make some money off the first song they get that people really want to buy and then can't do it because it is being pirated?

CHUCK D. Number one, I am telling every artist to be realistic and start from the bottom up. You get fans one by one. And also you figure out ancillary areas. I have been involved in the Silicon Valley areas as far as entertainment is concerned for the last I guess 4 to 5 years, and just recently we have designed a model with a few companies and specifically one unnamed company that has come up with a signature MP3 format which still would allow the public to get it for free but still would generate income to the artist and to the company.

I am not going to give that in front of Congress today because I am not the president of that company, but, you know, I mean I do work on this as an artist, and as an artist I have to explain a way that artists can eventually get paid. But, number one, I would like to see artists get into the game. See, the music business is probably choosing 2 percent of the artistry that is out there. So what does that mean for the other 98 percent, that they can't participate?

At least in sports you have a high school kid play on the school basketball team. There is no infrastructure in music at all. It just happens to be there is this big company, I have got money, I see something I like, and I am going to pick you, and I choose you. So for the first time a structure can be built where, if the companies are at the top and they have the top dollar, they can see a level of recruitment rise to the top. So this is something where the doors are open for them to participate, as opposed to being on the outside waiting for somebody to anoint them or select them.

And I think, you know, I have—I think we have about 1,200 artists on Rapstation.

John Hee, if he is still here, and you know, he has no complaints. He is trying to—he is in control of his destiny, and he is looking upwards.

Nobody wants to see the big guys destroy those companies, but they want to be able to see a fair game out there. So I think what this has done has leveled out the playing field where it is a fair game and artists can at least look forward to areas of business like joint ventures instead of one-sidedness. Hey, you get 10 percent, and they will say—I used to ask the question, why would I get 10 percent on my contract? And a lawyer told me, well, because nine out of every 10 artists fail, Chuck. That is why you get 10 percent. I said, what has that got to do with me? I am successful.

So, you know, you will see a change in the rules this century, and I don't think you will see anything go away. You will just see a lot of adaptation.

Chairman TALENT. I recognize the gentlelady from New York. I appreciate the Committee's patience.

Ms. VELÁZQUEZ. Chuck, can you give me an example of any recording artist who has successfully marketed themselves through the Internet without a label behind them?

CHUCK D. Well, first of all, if I am going to talk about myself, and I used to be on the other side, it wasn't just through records or music. I had like the first full downloadable album ever last year, and the whole key is I made the record for nothing.

Mr. SILVERMAN. I think she means from scratch, a new artist.

CHUCK D. I had artists along with me who made money off their materials and off their exposure by me putting them on tour in different countries around the world. They weren't able to do that before. On Rapstation.com we have 1,200 artists who are finding ways to expose their art in different area where they are finding ancillary areas to actually make money.

Well, money comes from—okay, I have a copyright, and I am going to stay at home and make sure that this record goes out there and just makes me money. I think that template is over with. I think now it is up to the artist to find nine or 10 different ways and say, okay, I have got this one song. Hey, Tommy Boy, can I actually get this one song on that compilation so that you can sell out there in the marketplace while I have made 30 other songs and it is doing its other work or whatever or what might not sell?

So you will see a new paradigm of artistry come about this. You won't see the lazy artist anymore, Tom, the lazy artist who wants to stay home and not work. It is over, because you have a million artists out there.

You have artists like John Hee, who moved here from Cleveland, who took—he took advantage of the whole Ohio market, moved here to D.C., is now taking advantage of this whole market here and actually getting his music around. He is a true Internet artist right back there. And he wants to go up, but in the past he couldn't even get in the music game. He would have to send a demo. And demos, you know, 95 times out of 96 times will sit up in the office and never would get listened to, and he would have a hard time getting in the game from Cleveland.

Mr. SILVERMAN. But the answer to her question really is that no artist has broken from the Internet without assistance of another person or other exposure from somewhere else.

CHUCK D. That will come, because what you are going to have is more exposed areas.

Ms. VELÁZQUEZ. But to answer my question, it hasn't happened?

Mr. SILVERMAN. Hasn't happened yet.

Mr. DUBE. MP3.com claims to have a couple of artists that make a living selling CDs through that site, maybe one or two. They are not household names, but they are making disks in a way that you don't have to sell very many to break even and to make money from it.

CHUCK D. You got people that sell a million records, but it takes them $7 to $8 million to sell a million records, and they are not making a profit. So, I mean, how much, you know, how does that idea work?

I mean, increasingly—what got me out of the record business in this old model is the fact that, you know, I would have a record and then they would tell me that, "Chuck, it is going to cost you about $750,000 in order to get the record played on radio." And I would say, "well, I have got a good record." You know, I have got a good record regardless, so why have I got to go through that political red tape to get my record played? It sounds like a whole bunch of hogwash to me. I want to create something that destroys radio. You know, if they are going to red tape me out——

And the same thing with television. If you don't have a $250,000 to $400,000 video, you can't get your video seen on MTV. So what does that do to the small business person? That is not right.

Ms. VELÁZQUEZ. You answered my question. Thank you.

Mr. Silverman, there has been occasion when I have purchased the same music in several formats—CD, cassettes and albums; and I assumed that the artist is receiving a royalty as a result of that. In these instances, the artist has received a royalty several times over as a direct result of the technology enhancements. My question is, is MP3 technology driving the music industry or is the industry driving technology? In other words, has the music industry in some small way helped create its own Frankenstein in Napster through the ability of users to obtain free music?

Mr. SILVERMAN. Well, it is a complicated question. Because when CD came out, vinyl and cassettes would be replaced, so people would rebuy the records that they already owned, and so there was sort of a free ride for record companies. For a while, that helped them. Besides selling the new music they were selling the old stuff over again. That has stopped now, and that is one of the reasons for the lethargy in the record business now.

Could this be the same thing? Yeah. If a device comes out that I could put 12,000 songs on tomorrow and an easy way to download them for a reasonable amount of money comes out, I could do two things. I could take all my CDs and put them in my computer and spend 6 months copying them all into the hard drive or whatever on something that is the size of that little Walkman thing, and I will carry that around with me and have every song I like that I have ever had, that I have ever liked with me in the car, when I am jogging or at home in a thing the size of a Walkman. I think that is a beautiful thing. Do I want to rebuy all my music? If it is easier, I think people do what is easier if the price is reasonable.

So there may be a chance for the replacement again of CD collections. By just pressing a few buttons and saying I want these, you wake up in the morning, they are all downloaded. And they are also filed with names and artists' names so that whenever the song comes up they are that way, and I can program them at a party so I can get *Yo! Bum Rush the Show* and then I can have *Planet Rock* right after it. So I can have a jukebox.

The thing has all this programming capability that you don't really have even with CDs, but for 10,000 songs, we are only a few years away from that. So, you know, it might be that way. Some people say we are going to not own music at all anymore, we are just going to have cell phones that we plug——

You know, in Sweden, they are working on this model. They are calling it WAP, W–A–P. Because other technology that is coming, where you just put your headphones into your thing and some wireless system gives you the song you want to hear whenever you want to hear it. So I want to hear this song and every time I play it, it costs me a quarter, just like a jukebox, or 50 cents. I will just listen to whatever I want when I want it. If it is the Delphonics or if it is a record coming out tomorrow, I can just listen to it for the same price or it might be multiple prices. I don't know.

All we know is that nothing is going to be the same. It is the most exciting time in the history of the record business, I think, certainly in the 23 years that I have been in it. So I am really excited, and I see that it is a possible opportunity, but the opportunity only exists if the copyright can be controlled by the artist. And the artist's partner is the record company, and I don't want to talk about what the nature of that partnership is because that is a whole other——

CHUCK D. Tommy, you are honorable, like I said. It is not like you are Hillary here or the rest of the record companies, because they would get beat down.

Chairman TALENT. Chuck, given the venue, you ought to make clear which Hillary you are referring to.

Ms. MILLENDER-MCDONALD. Thank you so much, Mr. Chairman.

CHUCK D. Well, not the one that is running for Senate, but you know—and I am a good friend of Hillary Rosen. It is just that you said—you are protecting cats that really, you know, look at you as having a job, you know. You are protecting their interests, and their interests—you know, and I am not saying the guys in the record companies are shady or bad guys. I am just saying this has been a one-sided system over the last umpteen amount of years, and now all of a sudden the audience or the consumer has gotten to the technology first before the industry. Now the industry is begging government to help them out. You know, did the consumers beg government to help them out when the industry was high-pricing them?

So I mean it is the laws of nature that have just balanced out. It is like the guy that walks to the corner, and he has this gigantic bag of M&Ms, and he dishes them out one by one, here, here, here, and this guy——

Ms. VELÁZQUEZ. Mr. Chairman, I think I have consumed my 5 minutes.

CHUCK D [continuing]. The bag breaks all of a sudden, and there are M&Ms all over the corner. It is hard to tell them, no, don't pick that M&M up, don't pick that up. It is like it is all over the street.

Chairman TALENT. Is the gentlelady finished?

Ms. VELÁZQUEZ. Yes.

Chairman TALENT. All right.

Next, I will recognize another gentlelady from New York, Mrs. Kelly.

Mrs. KELLY. Thank you, Mr. Chairman.

You know, with the Internet, e-commerce explosion, this Congress has had to deal with lots of issues of security and privacy and taxation and infrastructure development. We are sitting here struggling with a lot of issues on not just your field but many fields, and I would like to ask each of you to answer just one question for me. If you could write legislation that would affect and protect small music labels and entrepreneurs, how would you write it? What would you do to help protect yourselves?

CHUCK D. First, I would like to be able to say that everyone would have the opportunity to become a small record label.

Mr. SILVERMAN. You don't need legislation for that. They do have the opportunity.

CHUCK D. Now they do.

Mrs. KELLY. What would you do to protect the small record labels, the artists?

Mr. SILVERMAN. First of all, I think that it is possible that the judiciary can deal with the issue based on the laws that are currently on the book. If new legislation were necessary, you know, it would be hard to write it that would protect only the small business, but you would want a level playing field for sure so that no economy of scale would give an unfair disadvantage in the creative process to somebody who had more money which to some extent is the case right now.

For example, you know, because of economies of scale, those four majors own slots on radio stations and thus on the chart. I can't break in and I can't get my record that is worthy of getting played because I don't have the flow.

Chairman TALENT. Explain what slots—you referred to that several times.

Mr. SILVERMAN. Radio's top 40 radio station plays 40 records. They play in the top 10 those records are getting played 50 times a week or more. If you look at every radio station in the country, the top 10 records, 99 percent of their records they are playing on their entire play list are major label records. They are not from this 31,000 selection. They are from the 7,000 selection.

Part of the reason is the big companies have, you know, so much flow of product at such a high level and they are spending so much money that they have special relationships with independent promoters, they have special relationships with the radio stations themselves in terms of how much advertising that they can spend. So the cream doesn't necessarily get to rise to the top.

I am saying the same thing that Chuck has been saying, because an independent label and an artist are so close in what our concerns are. And as I have grown as a label I can see it from the major's perspective, too, but I have always fought for systems that will give us a level playing field.

I don't believe an independent label has the same shot to get a record played on the radio that a major label does because they have a guy who goes into every station every week and knows the guy and buys presents for his kids. We only go maybe twice a year. And, you know, we have to do it over the phone because we only have a few people in the field and we don't have one in every market like the big companies do. So that is an economy of scale, for example, where it shuts out things.

We actually haven't had that problem at MTV, and we certainly don't have that problem at BET. So on the video side we don't have that problem, but we find that problem is incredibly insidious at both black radio and pop radio.

Mrs. KELLY. Mr. Silverman, if I understand you correctly, you implied by your testimony just now that you feel we should let the lawsuits play out.

Mr. SILVERMAN. Yes.

Mrs. KELLY. That you feel that the laws that we have are on the books, that should be enforced, they are adequate enough, and you would not willingly go into this and rewrite law. Is that what I understood you to say?

Mr. SILVERMAN. Yes. I think that would add another level of confusion. I think the consumer and businesses are already confused. You know, the dust has to settle. Like Chuck said, no one knows what's going to happen next.

So if we wrote laws now they probably wouldn't be sufficient in 2 years because we don't know how it is going to shake out. We don't know if people are going to want this or they are going to want it through their cell phone. There is a hundred ways we might get digital music. Like you said with Point Cast, a million things are going to happen. There are way too many variables to be able to write laws. We have to wait until there is more consistence and we can see how it is going to play out.

I think the only thing that is important is that Congress has to understand that intellectual properties have to be protected because it is probably the biggest—it is the biggest export of this country; and we cannot condone cultural piracy, which is a Napster, Gnutella or whatever kind of a model. That is a model that gives no credence to the concept that an artist or an artist and its partner, the label, could possibly own a copyright, and I think that is the one thing—it is just clarity that is necessary now. If Congress can understand that and if the judicial can understand that, there shouldn't really be a problem for very long. These entities will come, and they will go.

I can't believe that people are financing these companies because, you know—basically, why don't you just finance an underworld operation? Because it is criminal activity.

Mrs. KELLY. Ric, do you have something you want to add to that?

Mr. DUBE. I think, in terms of the specific question, the independent labels are the ones best poised to benefit from what is going on right now. The Internet brings unprecedented exposure to those labels and those acts. It also means that a lot more labels are coming on board, so competition becomes fierce.

We are in a real awkward period right now. It sort of speaks to a question that was asked earlier whether the industry made its own bed here. It did, to a certain extent, but it wasn't conspiratorial. I think they were caught very much unaware, had no idea how quickly technology was going to be embraced and how quickly digital copies can be made and spread around. As a result, now they have got to figure out what they are going to do.

Right now, I think it is far too awkward to commit to any sort of legislation that would end up impacting things far down the road before we know how anything is going to pan out. What are consumers going to embrace? We have no idea. And how are the old world industries going to evolve their business models to take advantage of what people want.

Mrs. KELLY. Thank you very much. I thank all of you panelists for being here, because you are really giving us an insight that we would not have had otherwise.

Chairman TALENT. All right. I thank the gentlelady.

Let us at least begin Ms. Millender-McDonald's questioning before the vote.

Ms. MILLENDER-MCDONALD. I kudo, not kudo, just piggyback on the remarks that my colleague from New York has said. You have absolutely opened our eyes to something that otherwise would have been totally blinding to us. Because this concept was not privy to me, I should say; and I did not even know it existed. We are at a crossroads in this country, in this world, and it appears to me like, as I look at the MP3, you are working under the joint directions of international standards organization, international electrotechnology, everything that is international, which means everything is going global, everything is coming in from many fronts, many areas, many countries, and we have got to deal with that.

But in Congress, as you speak about laws, and perhaps we need to hold off until we find out where industry is going in this type of thing, we are makers of laws. We have to abide by laws, and those laws are on the books. Ofttimes, they are sometimes an infringement on rights or deals or the laws—the laws do not bring about competitive environments. And it appears to me like the laws that we have on the books have been as such where it is choking those who want to be innovative in their thoughts and their thinkings and want to move from areas that have been so restrictive.

And I say this because, as I look at you and look at what you have brought into the music world and how you are causing artists to have other directions for creating climates for selling their wares, then we need to look at the laws that might be restrictive for your doing that, especially those that are, I guess, promulgating the lawsuits that we have here.

But my question to you is, what do you feel is a level playing field and how do we—you know, what is the level playing field here?

Mr. DUBE. I think one way to look at a level playing field is in terms of copyright law. The World Intellectual Property Organization wants to make as many countries as possible ratify a treaty that would bring some sort of similarity, resonance to copyright law across the world. The issues that we are talking about are not domestic issues. They are worldwide issues. And if every country adopts different sorts of copyright laws to protect what is going on, there will be even more confusion than there already is.

Ms. MILLENDER-McDONALD. I was about to say, until you open up these markets, can you then talk about that?

Mr. SILVERMAN. China is the biggest source of pirated CDs right now, and it is the army that runs the plants.

CHUCK D. Yeah, but there are no record companies in China.

Mr. SILVERMAN. There are.

Ms. MILLENDER-McDONALD. Oh, what a day this has brought about.

CHUCK D. What does this mean if I want to have my record company from Nigeria? Is that not a country that is part of the world? So how does this apply? I am a worldwide person. I am heading to London tomorrow. I deal with the world. I just don't deal with the U.S. Of A.

I would like to know that my music is getting around now because of the Internet. Whereas I had a contract that said they would get it around and exploit my work through a company that said they could get it around but couldn't get it around and let me go to Nigeria and worry about that. Let me go to China and figure that out. Because I will be damned if I am letting the company say they went to China and not pay me for it.

Ms. MILLENDER-McDONALD. Well, Mr. Chuck.com, see, you are thinking global, and a lot of us aren't there yet. We are beginning to be and have that concept, but we are not—some of us are, but some of us aren't, and this is where I suppose conflicts are coming in.

What do you perceive—I mean, when I hear the whole concept of artists can go on-line, but where does that put that artist if he or she needs those traditional entities like distributor, whatever the promotional things are to promote your business? Is that not the traditional way by which you move your record on the Internet now?

CHUCK D. No, ma'am. It is a whole new thing happening. The Internet has allowed global exchange and global communication with a lot of people that want to be able to get in the game of entertainment music.

You have promoters that are in the Eastern Bloc that want to do hip hop, and they want to figure out how they can involve themselves or how they can get a group over into Prague or how they can get somebody over in Ghana. And now this interaction is creating a parallel industry to the industry that has existed before but just was really, you know, held to a domesticated situation. So these new understandings have to also be equipped with people that understand how this process is going down or how the radio station—how can I play something on Internet radio and it actually is listened to at the same time in Korea that it is listened to in East St. Louis. This is all new.

Ms. MILLENDER-MCDONALD. The only thing I want to say in ending my statement is that competition is what has been the norm. You are stating that competition by the mainstream music industry has kind of circumvented some of what is going on by the Internet, but then what happens when yours take on fire and the mainstream then becomes more dormant or can we expect that?

Mr. SILVERMAN. Then he will be the mainstream.

CHUCK D. But the thing about it, if you have got a million people all participating in the mainstream it is a better situation than what exists now. You have got four companies, soon to be three, making all the determination on what goes down. That is wrong.

Ms. MILLENDER-MCDONALD. So you are saying that this really opens up a better competitive type of environment?

CHUCK D. Yes, and Tom knows. It is like he is pressured into having one of his top groups have to do a $500,000 video, where if he doesn't have the flow why does he have to do a $500,000 to get it on MTV standards? What is good is good. It is not based on the money you spend, but the money is based on the corporate game of how they operate.

I don't want to be privy to be none of that. I want to be able to say, well, I have X amount of artists with me and what we present is good and we just want a fair chance to compete. And what Napster has done is just say, hey, you know what, it has created out of that limitation that existed before. So I mean, you know, what has come up out of this is that there is a lot of independent people who are now participating in the music business. And you know, of course somebody said, well, they are taking it or they are doing this for free, you know. Now they are in the music game, and this is the situation.

Ms. MILLENDER-MCDONALD. Mr. Chairman, thank you so much for such an innovative hearing.

Chairman TALENT. We have to break for the first vote today on China trade, and so we will come back in about—we will try and come back in 15 minutes with—Mrs. Bono will be next.

[Recess.]

Chairman TALENT. Could I call the Committee to order, please? If the witnesses could take their seat, please.

When Mrs. Bono returns, I will recognize her, but I had a couple of questions, and I thought I would take advantage of this lull to ask them.

Really I am pursuing, following up on what I asked before, to some extent pressing your imaginations. Tell me what this market is going to look like and let me pose an assumption here that may or may not be correct. Let us assume for a second that either the Congress and the courts do not have the will or do not have the ability to control the free flow of this art through the Internet, so that, as a practical matter, a person who is willing to do it can legally or illegally get somebody's music—or let us take the next step, get a motion picture, you know, get the next other piece of art over the Internet.

Now, what then will you be selling? Because you are the one in this, you are still selling at bottom, yet you are selling convenience of access, but you are still selling the right to this music. And, yes, there is some piracy and the rest of it, but there is still a lot of value to holding the license to that music.

If we can't protect it for you, what will you—let me give you an example of a market that was supposedly going to seed that was a problem. The satellite TV companies were able to pipe in to people who had the dish the local network programming so that you didn't have to watch the 10 o'clock news on the local network anymore, you got it over the satellite, or you got Denver's news if you were living in St. Louis or something, which threatened to just crumble this property interest that the local stations had. And Congress was able and desired to stop that because you could control the satellite companies.

Tell me, is the technology going to get to that point? And, if so, what is it you are going to sell to people, Peter?

Mr. HARTER. I am pretty confident that existing copyright law will be enforced effectively in some way that is fair to consumers and benefits artists.

Chairman TALENT. Let me press you on that. Because won't the technology be there? I mean you hit Napster, it is still out there, the software is still out there.

Mr. HARTER. It sure is.

Chairman TALENT. And if you take a consumer—in many instances, somebody buys a house and they happen to be still hooked up to the cable even though they haven't paid for it. What are they going to do, call the cable company and come out and say, you know, cut us off because—some people will, a lot of people won't. So assume that they can't. I mean, does this mean the end of the legitimate music business?

Mr. HARTER. I think if you look at Napster and its traffic, the amount of content available in Napster is highly unreliable and varies, based on what I said before, on the number of people logged on to Napster. And all of the tens of millions of Internet users out in the world, a very small subset can even access Napster effectively. You have to have a broadband connection to really be able to download music.

I mean, here Dwayne demonstrated downloading music. It is because there is a fast connection here. And we have this critical problem of the digital divide where people don't have access to the net, let alone to a fast connection.

Most of the Napster traffic—if you analyze the IP address, the Internet protocol address, most people on Napster are coming through cable broadband networks, not DSL, no satellite not yet. And I have talked to other broadband players about Napster, and they are trying to understand why this traffic is on their network. Because if all this music, all these big files are going back and forth and they are not making money on it and it is potentially an infringement issue that could go upstream back to them and it diminishes the quality of service—because if I am hogging the network——

Too, some of these TV commercials on TV, Pacbell in California advertises their broadband network to compete with cable. Because of cable's infrastructure if you are on the network all the time, your neighbor, he can't access the network as quickly. They call them web hogs. And DSL is apparently a different architecture you can access more quickly.

I think this is really a small, small problem. It has got a lot of press that has kind of magnified it in way that is very interesting, very amusing.

So if you look at the tantamount of users of Internet out there, only a small, elite population of broadband networks have access to Napster. And will it spread beyond that? Well, Napster doesn't work all that well, frankly. It is an unreliable supply.

And if Napster goes away because it has competitors—there is Listen.com. They are a legal competitor. There is Scour Exchange funded by Michael Ovitz in Hollywood. There is Gnutella, this rogue program from AOL. These things are very hard to use, and they are not going to transfer well into the mass market.

Chairman TALENT. So you are saying that we are going to end up, if we are halfway smart about it and don't panic, that we can have our cake and eat it, too? We can have reasonable protection for artists' exclusive ownership and anybody they make a real deal with and also be able to fully exploit the Internet for the benefit of the consumer and for new artists? You think that we will be able to control this enough so we can eliminate, you know, what all of us would agree are real abuses of people's right to profit off their creativity? You are just denying the premise of what I am saying?

Mr. HARTER. I think the DMC is working fine to level the playing field. Our business, EMusic, proves that, where consumers get cheap access to great music from independent labels and artists, the small guys, and we make it fun and affordable.

Piracy has always been in our industry, just like credit card fraud is out there. It is a part of doing business. And I think people are really getting too wound up on Napster because they have yet to show what their business model is. How are they going to pay their employees? They have got venture capital funding but how are they going to build revenue? And then these lawsuits are going to cripple the company. It is a mystery to me where they are going to go. They are going to be Point Cast.

CHUCK D. I think there will be more music sold than ever. And like I talked about previously, the Blockbuster analogy, you know, people you know still have blinking VCRs, and they can tape off of the television, and they still go to Blockbuster to rent the movie that came on Showtime that they saw that they could have taped. It is still sophisticated on the computers, and that is why I look at, you know, downloadable distribution and file sharing as the new radio. It is the new radio for this century or I should say this decade and—or at least this first 3 or 4 years, and now it is radio across the planet, and as this technology gets better and better it will expose more people to more music from more places.

Now, like I said, the domination of just four hands in the pot, I think that has just got to be split and shared. So I think, yes, you need a Tommy Silverman and a Tommy Boy who will look across the terrain. And, matter of fact, it gives us A&R guys credence to say, well, instead of checking out a room full of CDs, tapes and decks, now I can go to a bunch of sites and see who is doing what and pick the best minor league home run hitter and see if they can do their thing in a major.

And I just think the price of music will come down. I think the contracts of artists will actually be, you know, you will see the thousand dollar artist deal. I just think that with parity and everything across the board you will see a lot of different changes.

Do I think it is healthy? Yeah, I think it is healthy. I mean, because I looked at the music business for the longest amount of time, and I never saw anything that quantified who was better than the other. It was never that competitive field and especially in rap music. It was just like a bunch of guys live around New York so the A&R guys will pick a bunch guys that lived in the area. Where rappers were coming out of Houston and Cleveland and now Nigeria, but these guys wouldn't get signed because they wasn't within the eyesight.

Now you have got all these business models that are coming up, and I think people have to start from dollar one. They have to be able to make their art for little or nothing. They can make it for little or nothing with the new technology that allows them to make this. So the CD has just become part of our language for the last 20 years. It is not like people were talking CD in 1948.

So when these changes take place and take about, you know, we have to figure out, you know, how you go about making that art without spending beyond your means, and I just think it got silly for a while.

Chairman TALENT. And will deliver to people high quality music for less than 17 or 19 dollars that the CD—when I buy a CD as a gift or something to somebody, I am looking at this thing and I think to myself, how do the kids who really enjoy this music, how do they afford it? They can't buy 17 or 19——

Go ahead, Ric.

Mr. DUBE. I am just going to say, labels charge as much as they do for records because they release so many that fail, and to a certain extent successes have to compensate for a lot of the failures.

One of the ideas you are asking before, what will they sell, one of the things they can sell is just a terrific experience. If they can package a music experience on-line that is better than what Napster or Gnutella or any illegal forum provides, people will pay for it. Our research shows that people would be interested in paying for it. How would they? Well, maybe a subscription fee.

Right now, we know that 32 percent of college students said they spend less than $10 on music monthly. If you get some subsection of that group to commit to spending $15 a month on an all-you-can-listen-to subscription, whether it is streamed or downloadable, whatever, you have just expanded that section of the music market. So maybe it is time for the music industry to think, well, maybe it is not just about selling by the song or by the album, by the month, how do the consumers want to consume it, and give them that experience.

The other way to look at it is, in terms of artists, who if they make a buck and a half or two bucks on a CD sale on an $18 CD, that is a pretty wild margin. If you look at what they make from

a performance, people will always want to go see a live performance. They make far more money on a concert ticket. There are
some musicians out there right now, top name acts, who are perfectly happy to let kids swap the music for free because they know
it is putting asses in the shows and you make a lot more on the
concert ticket.

So that brings up the question, maybe, should music be free?
Could music be like network television where everyone is invited
to come along and corporate sponsorships and commercials and
things like that bring in the money? Maybe that could actually ex-
pand the music market. Maybe media companies wouldn't have to
take a hit on this.

Chairman TALENT. I recognize the very patient gentlelady.

Mrs. BONO. Thank you, Mr. Chairman.

First of all, I want to commend you for holding this hearing. I
was talking about this issue and these sorts of issues to some of
my colleagues not too long ago and saying we ought to get together
and at least begin a dialogue on where we are going, where the
music industry is going, and try to foresee some of the problems
that we are already hearing about here today. Of course, copyright
issues, I think are the most paramount among all of them.

But I wanted to say that my background in the music industry
is interesting, and I understand it somewhat, not as well as I
should or as well as I would like to. But beginning in the '60s and
moving on until today for various reasons—and I have a lot of
friends who are in the business, I am trying with the best of my
abilities to understand where we are going and what you are trying
to do, Chuck. It is hard, and I am listening, and I want to learn
and understand where we are going.

But I want to say something, Tom, to you about what you said
earlier—and I also just want to let you all know that a friend of
mine is here—and he is an artist, and I am happy that he is here
and listening to this dialogue. I have watched some of the frustration he had with his label as well. Not too long—it was very funny.
They just cut a new record, and I asked him if I could hear it. Oh,
no, no, no.

It is back to your comment about nobody wants you to hear it.
Nobody will let you hear the music any more. He said, no, no, no,
I won't let you hear it. And I said, you know what? I have a top
secret national security clearance, and you won't let me listen to
your record. I had to prove that I had that before I could even hear
it.

Understanding where the industry used to be, we used to have
masters, and now everything is a master, correct? Everything,
every file except for an MP3 file, because it is somewhat less—although it is not audible to the human ear, it is not a master file.
It is not anything quite as good as master, but basically you want
to control your masters somehow. Is there a way that you can do
what you are doing and go right to the Internet but artists who
want to be on labels and be protected—can have a dual system
where people are happy to be with their label and continue on that
way, you can go your way and can we have a dual system of music
that would exist?

Mr. SILVERMAN. More than dual, probably be seven or eight different options.

Mrs. BONO. Well, basically by dual I would mean those who care about their own copyright protection and those who don't. I know that Chuck, for instance, has permitted his material to be on the Internet. But at the same time, as I understand you have a couple of lawsuits pending against Bad Boy Records and St. Ives beverages because they have used your music without authorization. There is always a fine line.

CHUCK D. But it was defamation of character in both instances. It wasn't just uses of the music for their purposes. The St. Ives was a malt liquor company that used my voice, and I disdain the uses of malt liquor and other elements by corporations amongst the black community so I definitely took them on that. And the other one was, the Bad Boy situation, the 10 Crack Commandments record which endorsed crack with my voice all through it. So those were the two instances.

Mrs. BONO. Good for you.

Mr. SILVERMAN. Let me ask him a question. I am going to cross-examine the witness here. Do you mean if it wasn't that and they were just using your copyright to make money for themselves you wouldn't have had a problem with that?

CHUCK D. Well, being that they was major corporations, I have got problems with major corporations definitely tapping into me.

Mr. SILVERMAN. He was making a lot of money——

CHUCK D. I have been sampled, Tom, by millions of people. I don't have a problem with that because me as an artist—and this is just something I just hold to myself—me as an artist it is like, okay, boom, I will make art, and I will keep making art. I have got five studios, so maybe that has something to do with it. I wouldn't necessarily want another artist to adapt and take on my beliefs, but if somebody defames me as far as my opinion, oh, yeah, I am going to try. Because I can't go to them and beat them down because that is illegal. So you know, my manager says this is something that you should do.

So, you know, those were the two instances where I actually sued. I have been sued like crazy.

Mrs. BONO. Any public figure gets sued. That is, unfortunately, a given in this day and age.

But reclaiming my time a little bit here—and, Tom, I appreciate that you would like to be a Member of Congress and ask questions, but if I can do it now. I think this brings up a great issue, though, of realizing that these things have far-reaching consequences. Two years ago we had a major fight in the Judiciary Committee about these sorts of things, with the restaurants broadcasting music and to what level could they do it without paying royalties.

So these things do have far-reaching effects. These things need to be thought out carefully, and I don't want to see—and I understand again your frustration with record labels and have had them myself, but I don't want to see the artist throw out the baby with the bath water. I think we have to recognize there has to be a fine balance between artist and consumer, and we have to strike that balance.

CHUCK D. Excuse me, Congresswoman, the only thing I was saying pretty much before was that these changes wouldn't have come about if it wasn't for the technology forcing the hand, and the technology has forced the hand so now this is being dialogued where before it was just like—this truly was an old boys' network, and it was dominated by a select few and still is, and they are the ones that is crying now.

The RIAA has sent Tommy Silverman. The four major company guys are not here, and they are screaming the most because they played musical chairs with stockholders' money and all of a sudden they gutted these companies out, they stuffed the money in their pocket, and they are jumping out trying to play three sides of the fence. And, at the same time, don't say that you are protecting the copyright for the sake of artistry because the copyright pretty much is controlled by the labels at the end of the day.

You know, there is an artist you know that could exist in the 1950s whose masters and copyright was soaked up and bought long after they had moved on, and they really don't know what is happening with their copyrights or works of art, either, within the legitimate system.

So it is very easy to point out an illegitimate system as it is being formed, but how about this system that has existed that still hasn't paid Screaming J. Hawkins or many of the black artists that existed in the '40s and the '50s and the '60s who were exploited with bad contracts and who still—to this day, works are still being sold and they have yet to see a dime?

Because you know it is easy for somebody to say, oh, you haven't recouped the expenses that we divvied out to you. I had a lawyer tell me, said, "Chuck, you are not going to see a dime from Universal because you haven't recouped because we spent X amount of money on your behalf" and I am like saying, "ain't that something." I mean, I would like to actually have the money, don't spend it in my behalf and then charge me and say I ain't never seeing no money again.

Mrs. BONO. I don't want to be adversarial here, but maybe I am misunderstanding the advance system. There are advances given to artists by the record company and then you don't actually pay that back, do you?

CHUCK D. And money that is spent in your behalf you end up paying back.

Mrs. BONO. The label asks you to pay back?

Mr. SILVERMAN. It is recoupable but not returnable, if that is what you are asking.

Mrs. BONO. Mr. Chairman, may I have one additional minute?

Chairman TALENT. This is an interesting line. Go right ahead. But what is recoupable but not returnable?

Mr. SILVERMAN. Means if I give an artist $100,000 to make a record, they take the $100,000 and spend it and we never put the record out because it turns out really bad or they never finish the record, we don't get that $100,000 back. It is 100 percent our risk. If we sell a million records we can take out of their royalty payments the $100,000 and we get that back. That is called recouping the $100,000.

Mr. DUBE. You can dock their pay, but you can't make them write you a check.

CHUCK D. I give you a case in point. My first artist contract was 7 percentage points, 7 out of a hundred. I am being real brief because it is a crazy mathematics, but I made my first album for $17,000. That record to this date has sold over a million copies——

Mrs. BONO. That was your best album?

CHUCK D. No—at varied price ranges of wholesale prices and retail prices. And also it also brought in international figures that, you know, you would have to really send a team of accountants to comb out the money that that corporation had made.

Now, when they actually go into the area of recoupment, it gets into a gigantic mathematical quagmire that maybe myself as a fighter can go into, but not every single artist had the wherewithal to actually do this. So the amount of change that they have that has been split out of the glut of greed of pockets that have been stuffed along the way is astronomical. And so when the companies actually claim they have lost or are losing money you have to kind of like—guess okay, where—and where you gain money in all these aspects.

So I am not giving into that whole conversation, because that is neither here nor there, but I am just saying, in the level of business and in the level of artistry, when you hear the corporations talk about protecting copyrights and artistry, no, they are into protecting their masters that they own and the copyrights that they have taken control of, and that is their biggest concern.

Mrs. BONO. Sort of changing gears here and going another way, again, when you sell over the Internet, and you talked about technology that will allow you to pay per download or whatever to earn the money on that, but at this point in time, are you earning money or does an artist on the Internet earn money from eyeballs or from advertising hits, from people buying spots there?

CHUCK D. That will come about. We will have ancillary areas in all of the above. What we do at Rapstation is we set artists up with their own sites where they are able to sell goods and merchandise through the sites directly to them, 100 percent, without us being a middle person.

Mrs. BONO. So are we then at the risk of commercializing music here? My fear—and I have a degree in art history. I know it is sort of strange, but at the same time I do believe in the artists heavily. I spent 5 years studying this and married to one and all of that, but are we now at the risk of commercializing music? Will we see one day product placements in song, where you are paid by Coca-Cola to sing——

CHUCK D. If a song is sold for one red cent, it is commercial. My whole thing is like this, if the artist has to survive and the traditional way is outdated, then ancillary areas have to step up. You know, if a person makes a song and it is legitimate for Coca-Cola or whatever to pay them a million dollars, then that artist makes a living. You have got these companies out there that say, hey, we want to be able to trigger our products. How does Seinfeld get paid? We don't pay for Seinfeld when we turn on the TV. He is getting paid from somewhere or somebody. So is television commercialized?

Mrs. BONO. I am sorry, maybe I have given a bad description of commercial here. Again, I guess I think more in two-dimensional art form where—a painting versus a soup can label or something like that.

CHUCK D. I think art is subjective.

Mrs. BONO. That is my point, are we at risk somewhere down the road of hurting an art form because people——

CHUCK D. We are at risk by keeping it within three hands, truly.

Mrs. BONO. I am not disagreeing with you.

CHUCK D. I know.

Mrs. BONO. If nothing else—and thank you, Mr. Chairman, for the indulgence of allowing me so much time. But I believe, if nothing else, that what you are doing should serve as a very loud wake-up call to the record companies. And I know tomorrow in the Intellectual Property Subcommittee of Judiciary we have a hearing on the work for hire issue; and it is interesting because it is so diverse, these two issues, yet they are similar as far as looking back at protecting past copyright and moving forward here.

CHUCK D. I disagree that companies should have a copyright and then own it forever. They have talked about expanding it to 56 years, of owning a copyright for a situation, and I am like, okay, you know, I could see that if it is a joint venture, but if it is not a joint venture, you know, business to me, it is like something that you work out. The music business has not been music business. It has been music employment.

Chairman TALENT. I think Mary can answer this, but we lengthened the time you can own a copyright, didn't we? That was for Mickey Mouse because Mickey Mouse was going to enter the public domain and that was considered to be not viable, anybody could use Mickey for whatever they wanted.

Mr. DUBE. In response to that question, the way you are talking about commercializing music, I think we will see that. I think downloadable music, digital music in general, really, the ease of the format means that pretty much anybody can be a music company if they want to be. And if that means that when artists' contracts end, Procter and Gamble or Coca-Cola company wants to put in a bid on a popular artist, that they become associated with that product. Just like television in the '50s. Everybody knew that Bob Hope was Texaco or Dinah Shore was Colgate, Palmolive, whatever. We could have that same sort of close association.

Now, we talked about the risk of cheapening music or kids in particular have pretty good bullshit detectors. If they put out crap, they won't embrace it.

Mrs. BONO. I disagree with that.

Mr. DUBE. Art is subjective.

Chairman TALENT. If the people who buy the music don't want you to talk about Pepsi, or don't want you to talk about Pepsi if you are getting paid to talk about Pepsi, you won't be able to talk about Pepsi, will you?

Mr. DUBE. On the other hand, artists already are subsidizing their incomes with corporate sponsorships. If you have a real big, expensive tour and there is no way you can make money on the ticket, that is the biggest reason.

Chairman TALENT. It is the reason Tiger Woods wears Nike, right?

Mr. DUBE. Exactly. We will see more of that with music.

Chairman TALENT. I thank the gentlelady.

Yes, Mr. Phelps, sure.

Mr. PHELPS. Thank you, Mr. Chairman. Just a few questions.

So I can be straight in my mind, as a new member and somewhat involved in the music industry, if I understand, all of you do agree that the issue is not copyright protection. You all believe that there should be protection of copyrights for artists' work? Okay. I guess I hear Mr.—but I should call you Mr. D?

CHUCK D. Call me Chuck.

Mr. PHELPS. Chuck, I believe your message is that you are wanting anything in the natural order of things to work in this industry without too much regulation or any big attention being drawn to what is concerning Mr. Silverman, as long as the big boys who I guess have abused the system——

CHUCK D. Right.

Mr. PHELPS [continuing]. And the question I have is that people like you that emerge through that bad system, how are you successful, as opposed to some of these little guys that you are giving a break through the openness of this system now, what separates the men from the boys here?

CHUCK D. I don't know. I always rebelled the system while I was within the system. I didn't ask for a record label. I was recruited by Rick Rubin. I told Rick Rubin, who was then the head of Def Jam records, if I get in the music business I am going to change the music business, and we are going to work something out between me and you. And I worked it out with Rick Rubin, not Russell Simmons, not CBS. That was his relationship with them.

Mr. PHELPS. So this agreement you had that you described some time ago——

CHUCK D. My thing was to make rap music global music.

Mr. PHELPS [continuing]. $17,000 agreement that you mentioned a few minutes ago, even though that was not good for you, you thought that was all right to go ahead and proceed in the music business?

CHUCK D. I made the record for $17,000, and therefore I turned then to Rick Rubin who had agreements with the major record companies. His agreement was with the major record companies. He didn't have the best of all deals either. I think Tommy could attest to that. So, therefore, I understood the situation I was getting into. I had a goal to get into the music business——

Mr. PHELPS. For reforming it, evidently.

Mr. D [continuing]. To reform it, to get a lot of people involved in it, to stand up for a genre that was scrutinized, to try to be an ambassador for a genre, to try to make a global, cultural exchange out of the genre, to try to speak up for a lot of people from my community, and to try to tie this together into being a participant in the music business. And one thing led to another and certain things, certain ideas were reached. And there is still work to do, but don't think I came in the music business because I had my hand up just wanting to make a record. I was way past that.

Mr. PHELPS. So your view of this technology is sort of doing justice to what—the big guys have abused the system. It is a way of bringing them to their knees maybe?

CHUCK D. I wouldn't say that, but I would say that it is creating one of the biggest transitions ever in the world of music, and I think it needed it.

Mr. PHELPS. Because what I see in this is that—I know we are talking about one segment of the music industry which is a big one, but how do we not talk about all the other segments in the music industry, such as your licensing organization—I am an affiliate of BMI. What do we do about ASCAT, BMI, and what do we do about the radio stations because without those vehicles it doesn't matter what you produced? Who decides what the Top 10 is? Is it 10 people who get in the room and say this is what we will play or is it money flowing?

Mr. SILVERMAN. Up to now it has been record sales, and I know that SoundScan that tracks record sales will also be tracking downloads.

Mr. PHELPS. But record sales on the digital——

Mr. SILVERMAN. Both.

Mr. PHELPS. Right now it is?

Mr. SILVERMAN. They have just started tracking. They are planning to track all digital.

Mr. PHELPS. That could be deceiving in a way.

Mr. SILVERMAN. What?

Mr. PHELPS. About what really the public is wanting to hear?

Mr. DUBE. It has never mattered before whether a person bought something on a CD or cassette. Format was irrelevant. So in terms of singles which is the way most MP3 songs or digital songs are distributed, hopefully then it wouldn't matter. It would format agnostic.

Mr. PHELPS. Should we worry about BMI for them to collect their fee, for a rider such as myself to get their part before it goes out to the radio station or on disk?

CHUCK D. Like I say, you will see new paradigms being created. I remember one time this well-versed person working at ASCAT suggested that the mechanical rights for particular songs might go down or might disappear but the performance rights of a particular song might have to be adhered to with a downloading of a song on the Internet. You know a lot of this stuff is just proposed and it is guesses and people are trying to figure out which way this is going to lead to.

Like I said, I am a big proponent of at least getting people into the game and getting involved; and that is where this digital revolution has been, I guess, most rewarding. So when it comes down to your works actually getting exposed or downloaded, yes, maybe it could become a licensing issue. That is a sophisticated discussion for the average artist who is usually kowtowed into the industry and just told to make records and don't think about anything else.

I think what you will see what come out of this is a more educated artist, and like I said before, the lazy artist is over with. The guy who just wants to make records and just be dumb, those days are over with. It is not my calling. It is just like rain, it is going to rain on everybody, and technology is going to rain on everybody and this is what is going to happen. My whole thing is, Chuck D, how do you exist when it rains. Well figure out how I put up my umbrella and adapt in walking on water.

Mr. PHELPS. So you don't fear a Chuck D, Jr. taking your most cherished rap work and maybe doing a different twist to it?

CHUCK D. Sir, I have been sampled more than anybody. I don't have a problem with anything.

Mr. PHELPS. Elvis might have a little bit different to say about that if he was here. That is probably true now.

CHUCK D. Don't combine me with Elvis.

Mr. PHELPS. But you are talking about global, the Beatles I don't think were really the Beatles until they came to the U.S. of A, were they?

CHUCK D. But I don't see—we can't talk 1964 when we are in 2000.

Mr. PHELPS. We are talking about evolvement of an industry.

CHUCK D. But the industry is evolving. Over the last 5 years, it has evolved at greater levels than it has ever evolved. Would you agree? In the last 5 years, each and every month in the music business right now constitutes for a year that would have been in the seventies.

Mr. DUBE. At least.

Mr. PHELPS. Thank you very much.

Chairman TALENT. A very interesting line. Thank you. Mr. Davis has been very patient. I want to recognize him now.

Mr. DAVIS. Thank you, Mr. Chairman, and I want to commend you for calling this hearing. I know it sounds kind of exotic and in some instances erotic, but I think it is a very serious issue that we are exploring. It is a very complex matter, and I think the level of participation and the engagement that we have heard this morning is indeed quite enlightening.

I also want to thank each one of the panelists and commend them for their participation and appreciate very much the information that they have shared with us this morning.

I have two questions that will be kind of put into one, but Chuck, let me suggest that I commend you for what you are doing in terms of trying to expose in a way and take a hard look at what has happened in the industry and especially as it relates to artists. I have a large number of very personal friends who are, in fact, in the business. Foremost among them probably is also another elected official, Jerry Butler, whom I served with for several years on the Cook County Board of Commissioners, who is a very serious politician in addition to being a great artist dating back many, many, many years, and there are a number of other individuals as well.

You see, I hope that as a result of these kinds of discussions that not only will artists but also, Chuck, in the case of the impact that I think your involvement may have on many of your fans, that they too would realize that they don't have to take things simply as they are, that they too can be engaged and be involved, and while some of the art form itself, I can't suggest that I am so heavy into it, probably my age has something to do with that, especially when it comes to certain kinds of language and that kind of thing but certainly the effort.

The question that I really have for the entire panel is, are you suggesting in any way, shape, form, or fashion that maybe we ought to be looking at regulation of the use of the Internet as it relates to commercial property rights of any kind, I mean whether we are talking about music or whether we are talking about something else that can be pirated, used? I come from the City of Chicago; and, of course, if there is any way to pirate anything, there are people in Chicago who will find it. I mean, they will find it if there is a way; and the other part of that question, though, is also will use of the Internet result in an increase, decrease, or make any difference in the amount of money that is generated by the music industry?

CHUCK D. I would like to answer that, Mr. Davis. I would like to say that there is no quantitative method that says that the music business has lost money or will lose money. And looking at particular companies, and I am not trying to go there again, but looking at their wealth of catalog that they have, that they fail to exploit, although they have the rights, if somebody wanted to go get Jerry Butler's, *Your Precious Love,* from 1959 and they was going to the company that had that right to that master or that copyright and they couldn't find it in the store, the Internet serves as a perfect vehicle to get it across to them.

Now what is going to happen, instead of regulation of the Internet, I think a navigation process of the Internet might take place first to make this wealth of catalog which is obscured by I guess the red tape of retail not being able to fit it in their stores. One gentleman, I think it was Mr. Dube who said that you know an obscure song by a great, which might not be reprintable because they say it is not beneficial to press up 20,000 copies, you know, that one song that you probably liked from Jerry Butler in 1961 can be searched, researched, and found on the Internet. If there is some signature code and signature file on that MP3 which allows you to get that song, I think we are moving to that point.

Like I told everybody before, I am involved in a situation that still would allow the consumer to get the MP3 for free but moneys still be generated for that copyright. The Internet is the saving grace for the record companies because they are sitting on a wealth of catalog that they don't know what to do with. And understand this, this primarily is the biggest problem with the music business today, is that they are gigantic, but they don't have people equipped to handle the speed of technology, and they don't have the people that understand the wealth of catalog that they own. So they haven't even touched upon everything that they own because you have a lot of people who—it is not a job that is built yet.

I had relationships with Polygram before they merged with Universal or got absorbed, that is really what happened, but their catalog department which had a wealth of catalog and copyrights that they control, the Motown catalog, the ANM catalog from Herb Albert. The problem was—is that the heads of these companies were business people and they could care less about the art. But the people that were in the catalog departments were true music people that wanted to do things musically and also commercially with the music, but the overstructure on top of them wasn't sophisticated enough to give them the go ahead answer. So these are big corporations or multinational corporations, but the hand and elbow might as well be three miles apart.

So what you have got is the business changing, the music business still operating off a traditional model, with people that haven't had clearly defined jobs. So you want to talk about waste, there is waste because your good friend Jerry Butler has done hundreds of songs, and there is a listening audience that want to hear those hundreds of songs that cannot get those songs in the regular traditional marketplace. The Internet provides that opportunity.

Mr. DAVIS. Yes.

Mr. HARTER. There are some studies out there, and these are all preliminary, but they project on-line distribution whether it is by downloading or streaming will produce an additional amount of revenue for the music industry on top of what they are already selling, and a lot of people already say on-line distribution takes away from CD sales. I don't think that is credible. I think that is a bunch of hogwash. The fact is several billion dollars will be added to the revenue of the record industry and largely independents who comes to, like, my company because we are putting product on the market that could not easily get to market.

And then the back catalogue is an excellent point. Publishers tell me that over 50 percent of the art of the music ever created, produced is not on the market. It is not being monetized, it is not being put into commerce because retail space is too expensive. If you have a song from 50 years ago that will only ever sell 1,000 copies a year worldwide, you can't put it on a CD in a store. It is just inefficient. The retailer will lose their shirt on that kind of business process.

But the Internet, it doesn't matter. One copy or a hundred copies, it costs the same. You get a big server with millions of songs on it, different versions of the same songs, anybody in the world can come on the Net and download and pay for it. Or if you want to have a subscription-based service or use advertising to pay the artists then people can download for free. And you can charge a quarter for it, charge a dime for it, charge $1 for it, or charge $18 for it; but I don't think they will come to your site if you are charging those kinds of prices.

I think there is tremendous amount of money to be made for all kinds of art that is out there that many people haven't seen. All we get is Britney Spears it seems.

Mr. DAVIS. Either one of you?

Mr. DUBE. Yeah. I would say that right now in the same ways the stock market goes through correction periods, right now the price of music and entertainment in general is going through a correction period, and until the industry and the public can figure out what they want and how to make that happen, in direct response to the question, I would advocate no specific regulation other than to point out one more time that these are not domestic issues. Some of these are worldwide issues, and then there are treaties that exist to bring countries together. I think the U.S. laws are already WIPO compliant. I could be wrong about that but there is a lot of countries out there that have committed to ratifying the treaty that are not; and if we can help that, that is something that can be done.

Mr. DAVIS. Well, go ahead.

Mr. SILVERMAN. I just think pricing, it is difficult to talk about pricing, but pricing is really, it is about supply and demand, and demand in music is how much somebody wants a record. Somebody really wants a record, like a collector will pay 50 dollars for a 45 if they really want the record. A person who doesn't care about the record won't pay $2 for that same record or if even you offer to give it to them, because sometimes at our label, we get all these promos and stuff, and we leave a stack out there for people to take. No one takes them. The cleaning people won't even take them. No one wants them because they don't know about them, and MP3.com is like that, 60,000 tracks that people don't want.

You have got mom and pop playing a banjo and singing along. Everyone can have their record on there, great, I am published now, I am a record company. You know what, you go into Tower they have 50,000 titles. They have one of the biggest selections of any of the record stores, and people get choice anxiety, they walk out with nothing or they walk out with Britney Spears because they went in there because wow they have an obscure blues artist, wow, there is Ella Fitzgerald, Louis Prima, and all of these records are all around and they walk out with Britney Spears anyway which they could have gone to a store that only had 3,000 titles and walked out with.

Now you go to an environment that has a quarter of a million artists on-line, the people are even more confused, what do they do. It is just too much for people. A lot of people just want to say, okay, my kids, they want Britney Spears or Bloodhound Gang or whatever the hot record is because either they heard it on the radio or they saw the video, period. That is what the record business is going to be. Digital, analog, I don't care, people want to buy what they know and what everybody is talking about. They are talking about what they saw the video on and what they heard on the radio last, and that is irrelevant of whether there is an Internet or there is not an Internet.

Chairman TALENT. Regardless of whether there is an Internet, MTV is still going to tell everybody what to buy?

Mr. SILVERMAN. MTV and radio stations.

CHUCK D. I beg to differ because I think in 2 years, you know, the fact you would be able to see a video on call instead of seeing— I would love to see an Afrika Bambaata video. But why would I wait for them too? No, I would like to go to the Tommy Boy site and drum that up on real player and then whoa, Afrika Bambaata, or go to another name and say, wow, I want to be able to see that Naughty By Nature, *Feel Me Flow* video, and then you are seeing video on call and on demand which drives you right back to the product again. This is all new paradigms. But I am saying the average consumer is changing. And I will say that, yes, there is going to be tons of product out there. But you are going to have a billion people with access; and like you just said, with the cellular phone you are going to, like, say people are going to be in Kenya you know probably being able to say—you know you won't be able to sell the album to them for five or $10, they might be able to buy those albums for 30 cents Kenyan money. So it is going to add into a world pot somewhere. You are going to have an expanded global place. So you can have a lot of artists because you are going to have umpteen amount of expanded target audience.

Chairman TALENT. Okay. I will let Peter have the last word; and then if the gentleman is done, Mr. Sweeney will be next.

Mr. HARTER. To answer the gentleman's question, I don't think there is a need for regulation right now. Let us see how the DMC works out. I want to point out, there is another start-up business that is going to be, if not already is, the leading directory, the leading information location tool for music on the net. It is called Listen.com. Now, for the record, the five major record labels have invested in the company as Madonna's record label Maverick Records, and they power the search engine on EMusic's site, and they are a business partner of ours.

But what I think they are doing is helping people make choices. Where I go into Virgin Megastore in San Francisco, and they have listening booths and have a DJ spinning tracks, all to influence you to buy things, because buying music is largely impulse. Listen.com has a director of music. They have artists reviewing music saying this is what this music is and the career of this artist, this band, and hey, there is a need to know this artist was in this band and if you like this artist, this music, we suggest you like this because it is similar for these reasons. They inform the consumer. So instead of just buying what is flashed in front of you on the cycle, on MTV or the radio, you can actually learn more about the art, find out what makes the artists make that art and where they got the influences from and what is similar to it. So I like listening to Miles Davis, I want to find out why he went through a different stage of his career and who influenced him, like in the fusion age and the sixties.

Mr. SILVERMAN. You are an anomaly, too.

Mr. HARTER. I think that is changing.

CHUCK D. People want to be interactive instead of being programmed. I think we are going from a program marketplace into a marketplace that is being more and more interactive.

Mr. SILVERMAN. If that was true there wouldn't be a blinking 12 on everyone's VCR.

Mr. DAVIS. Let me thank the gentleman very much. You have shed a tremendous amount of light on a very difficult and complex subject, and I will certainly be using some of the components of it as I speak with young adults and as I speak with young people about not only the content of things but also what happens as we explore this whole question of who makes decisions in our country, and so I thank you very much, and thank you, Mr. Chairman.

Chairman TALENT. I thank the gentleman. As always his questions were gracious and enlightening; and I recognize another gentleman from New York, Mr. Sweeney.

Mr. SWEENEY. Thank you, Mr. Chairman. Let me say thanks to you and commend you on holding this hearing and thank the witnesses as well in what is turning out to be one of the most informative panels that I think I have ever participated with. It is kind of an interesting day. I missed some of your testimony, read a lot of it. This is a day that we are in Congress trying to balance the equities on how to make the world marketplace a freer place and how to deal with 1.2 billion people in China and all of the judgments you have got to make in that, and I am listening to testimony.

I have got to say, Chuck, I came in with some preconceived notions; and you have turned me because I think your message is about freedom, freedom of choice for people and the marketplace largely. And I understand what you are saying, Mr. Silverman; but I think in the end, we as a legislative body are always going to try to strive to find the way to give Americans greater access to whatever it is as consumers because it is the definition of what we have.

I have also learned, where I grew up if you don't know an awful lot about something you sit back and listen and are quiet and so I am going to do that, and in doing that, I am going to turn over my time, to yield my time to someone who knows a lot more about this than I do, and that is my colleague from California, Mrs. Bono. I thank you.

Mrs. BONO. I thank the gentleman for yielding. I have been in politics long enough if you can't dazzle them with brilliance, baffle them with something else. I don't know that I know that much more about this, and I don't want to be the one to stand in between Chuck D and a fish sandwich or a peach drink because I know this hearing has gone on for a while. I just want to ask one last question of Peter and that is, you are saying that this has not yet hurt CD sales, but isn't that a little bit unfair—not unfair. Wouldn't you say in 2 or 3 years as people become far more familiar with MP3 format that will change?

Mr. HARTER. I think it is true that the physical delivery system of music, whether it is buying through Amazon, have a CD shipped to your house, or going to a big store in person, big store or local store, chain, nonchain or mail order, that will always have a place. That won't be eliminated.

Mrs. BONO. But the ratio will change, CD sales are going to decline?

Mr. HARTER. If the market is $40 billion roughly today and if you bring all this content that is not on the market that Chuck and I have been talking about and independent artists break their music on their own or with small labels on the net, you are actually making money on content that was never in commerce in the first place. So the gross revenue of the industry goes from 40 billion to a hundred billion dollars or more, and some of that will be CDs, but I think a lion's share of that will have to be Internet because physical distribution is economically inefficient and defunct for a small niche market.

If there are 90 million Francophones on the planet, in Europe, in the former colonies in Africa and in southeast Asia and people have that common language and they want to give back to their roots French music, not many Americans are going to listen to French music, but somewhere else in the world, people want that French music, and say it is a Cajun artist in Louisiana and his family has roots back in France, I am going to download it from a Web site in New Orleans or wherever the server happens to be. Is that music going to get marketed in the major stores? Probably not because it won't sell in the volume necessary to justify that physical CD taking up precious retail space.

Mr. SILVERMAN. How are they going to know about it?

Mr. HARTER. Promotion on the Net.

Mrs. BONO. I hate to lose the respect of all four of you, but I just bought Britney Spears new album last week on Amazon.com for my 9-year-old daughter. So I hope you still respect me.

Mr. HARTER. My girlfriend likes Britney Spears, and we had an argument about that the other day. I lost.

Mrs. BONO. That is why you are here and she is not, right? My last question, and thank you, Mr. Chairman again. Something we haven't talked at all about and I am glad to hear us all say go slow in regulation, we don't need it now and let us go slowly as this evolves. I hate to bring up the big T word, but have y'all thought about what could possibly creep in the form of taxation here and what we do to avoid that?

Mr. HARTER. In preparing for this hearing, I talked to some very smart lawyers who actually listen to digital music. And they downloaded and I gave them players and they actually understand the technology and asked them if copyright law were not to be held by the courts or Congress to apply to Napster, what about State, local or Federal tax law? And there is the issue of whether barter or exchange taxes apply to Napster. And while Napster's business model is evolving, if it facilitates an exchange of commercial goods, which music is, between two individuals and they profit from it because they make money on the eyeballs, they trap the site in advertising and other marketing revenue streams, some interesting State and local or Federal taxes may be applicable to barter and exchange of music. If Napster is going to do commercial business with investors and shareholders and employees, people want to collect taxes for that kind of activity. I don't know if they thought about that issue. I am not sure if it really applies. I am not a tax lawyer, but it is an issue that needs to be raised.

Mrs. BONO. Thank you. Anybody else?

Mr. SILVERMAN. Who do you pay taxes to?

Mr. HARTER. I am glad you asked. We want to pay all the royalties to artists and rights holders, and if there are applicable taxes we will pay them. All our servers are in California, but if someone is going to tell me that they think we have a customer over in Europe—and we don't care where our customers come from. They pay by credit card, and the artist gets paid.

We are not going to invade the privacy of the consumer to find out where they consume the music. We are going to pay based on the country of origin of our servers, not the destination of where someone tells us that download occurs because that just requires us to become Big Brother and find out where you are when the music enters your ears. And I think there is some very large policy questions in terms of Internet law about jurisdiction, which country of origin, the server or the company or destination of where the consumer is.

This administration is split on the issue, and the Europeans want to move to a country of destination position. It is very controversial, and it applies to taxes and assessment of royalties. So that is going to be an issue that may impede small businesses because they can't afford to understand these issues or implement a solution.

Mr. SILVERMAN. Another example of what he is talking about that is not necessarily taxes. If I have a licensee in France that breaks my record in France and invests the equivalent of $100,000 in promotion to do that and I have a deal with EMusic and they sell 10,000 copies in France digitally, should the French company get a piece of that royalty because they are the ones who made it, like they got it on the MTV of France and they got it played on the radio stations in France, they are the ones who paid and invested in making the demand in that market, or should I get that?

I mean, that is a big question as well. Maybe a bigger question than France, and I think that I would have to say, yeah. I have to know where, if the records are being sold in France, I am going to have to share with it with my partner who helped to break it in that territory because they deserve it. Otherwise, if people aren't ordering from Italy because my guy didn't break it in Italy and they are ordering from France, why shouldn't he get it? It is clear that it was his responsibility.

I also have a study, I want to tell you about your prior question, that just came in today that I thought I should share with you because I would be remiss if I didn't. A new study came out today, a entertainment study with VNU, with SoundScan basically, which reveals on-line file sharing is the likely cause of decline in college market album sales. They actually—this was just released, and the study concluded that sales were down by 4 percent in stores within a 5–mile radius of 3,000 colleges. And stores near 67 schools that had banned Napster by late February had a greater sales decline of 7 percent over the past 2 years, and that is in light of record sales going up everywhere else. So this is the first actual study that has actually shown a connection between file sharing and sales drop offs.

Mrs. BONO. Thank you. Thank you, Mr. Chairman.

Chairman TALENT. Is that study of illegal file sharing or legal file sharing or both?

Mr. SILVERMAN. Well, it says, here is the quote, "It is now clear that the controversial practices of companies that provide directories and an easy interface to libraries of unlicensed music are, in fact, detrimental to the growth of the music business and those artists whom they claim to support. Record sales are up despite the widespread use of MP3, not because of it. These figures should put to rest the ongoing debate about the effects of on-line file sharing."

Chairman TALENT. I think it is probably, owing to this one gentleman who wrote me, and maybe the retailers in general to read this into the record, too. It is a letter from the man who owns Oliver's Record in Syracuse, New York, as a matter of fact. It says, "Syracuse University allows free access to Napster. In several interviews with the Syracuse newspaper, has stated that have no plans in firewalling Napster. My business has fallen off to about twenty percent of what it was before this started. I had not heard of it until the Christmas break when a young man came in and told us how great this new program was that allowed all students across the country to trade their music and then asked me, so, how long do you think you will be in business. And that kind of question can only come from the young. I didn't think much about it then since I had no idea what he was talking about. I then went on and tried it for myself and it is everything I thought it would be. As for Limp Bizkit's lame reply that people are just sampling the music before they buy, Oliver's has proved that that is totally off the mark. I just wanted you to know from someone at the lower end of the food chain. Thank you, Charles Robbins."

I guess maybe a closing question for you all. You have been very patient. And I want to wrap this up by 1 o'clock, and we are almost there. We have sort of—you all have told me, and I will accept on what you say, that you think that the law can effectively control the illegal on-line distribution of music. Will the legal distribution of it, Mr. Harter, end up in cutting out the retailer? I am not saying that that is necessarily bad, the economic change affects people, but is there going to be a place for people who still have music stores and sell CDs?

Mr. HARTER. I love this question. People have a life beyond their computers. They are not going to sit at their computers doing everything. They will be in Starbucks at a kiosk and buying music, and actually Starbucks sells quite a few CDs of their prepackaged compilations. And people love music and are going to get it where it is fun and less convenient. I think people in retail stores pretty well understand their customers and how to market to them and appeal to them to get them to buy something and induce them. So as Chuck was saying earlier, they have to adapt to the new market and piracy has been around just like credit card fraud has been around. It is the cost of doing business. I think everyone is going to be able to adapt in some way.

Chairman TALENT. That assumes price competitive products. One of the questions I have got is because there is significant overhead to maintaining a retail establishment, if you can get the stuff off the Internet and it is as good and you get it in the same form you would buy it, in other words, not like a book where there is some value in having a book, even if you can download it on a computer, you like to give it as a gift or whatever, I am wondering whether this may not be a line of business where Internet sales really will swallow up retail businesses.

Mr. HARTER. I think it is a bit of back to the future. Richard Branson, the founder of Virgin records, in reading his biography a while ago, when he opened his record shop he drew people in because from what the book said, they could smell pot in the record shop, hang out and listen to music all day, it was a lounge, and the longer you stay in the record store, the more likely you will buy more music. And I think now that we are kind of going back to the situation where you go to a Virgin Megastore, they have a coffee bar, a book shop, magazines, there is merchandising, there is a DJ playing great music, there are listening kiosks, or Borders. I think the retailers large and small will find very interesting ways to create a new customer experience.

Chairman TALENT. You are probably right. It comes down to value added, doesn't it?

Mr. SILVERMAN. And he is talking about the big stores. On the small business level, George's Music Room in Chicago and Rock and Soul in New York and these small stores, DJs are going to go there and people are going to go there who are regular customers because the people who work there know the music, know what they want and turn them on to new music.

Actually, the independent record store, they used to call disrespectfully the mom and pop stores, are actually doing better now against the Best Buys of the world even though they are selling things at full list price and competing at $17 for a CD than they were 5 years ago because they have realized that their niche is to know their customer in the way that no big store can ever know their customer. They have to put in espresso bars in order to compete and create an upbeat and entertainment destination for another reason. So I think that these independent stores are going to be less vulnerable except in the college area unless they are offering other opportunities like these guys might make up for it by selling blank disks.

Chairman TALENT. Part of the problem is not adjusting quick. There seems to be some consensus here that assuming we can protect against piracy to a reasonable degree anyway, on-line purchase or access to music is going to result in lower prices for consumers, access to a whole lot broader range of music, a fairer deal for artists over the long term and maybe breaking the control over the business that has heretofore been exercised by a few people. Is that a good way to sum up what you all think? Does anybody disagree with that?

Mr. SILVERMAN. Except it won't break the control of the media because they are the media. The same people who control the media own the record companies.

CHUCK D. That will break up because the expanded media exists in that parallel world of the Internet.

Chairman TALENT. When it is fractionalized enough. Thank you all for coming. The hearing is adjourned.

[Whereupon, at 1:10 p.m., the committee was adjourned.]

53

House Committee on Small Business

"Online Music: Will Small Music Labels And Entrepreneurs
Prosper In The Internet Age?"

May 24, 2000

Opening Statement of Chairman Jim Talent

Thank you for joining the Committee today for our hearing to discuss
the future of online music distribution models and the ways new
technology will affect smaller record labels and music acts. This is the
third in a series of hearings that the Committee has held regarding E-
commerce issues and one that is very timely. With so much of the
attention these days being devoted to the controversial music file
swapping software Napster, it is a good time to explore how issues like
piracy, as well as privacy concerns, marketing budgets, and the near
omnipresence of the World Wide Web, affect the bottom line of smaller
music entities.

The advent of MP3, which is essentially a file format that allows
computer users to download near CD quality music and audio files, has
made listening to music via the Internet a reality for many computer
users. The algorithms used to encode MP3 files compress the data to
convert a file that would take 40 minutes to download in regular CD
format just 5 minutes to download as an MP3 file. In order to attain the
smaller file size, this compression destroys some audio parts that will
never be reconstructed, which is why MP3 cannot reach exact CD
quality.

As more people have access to the Internet and MP3 files there have
been various concerns voiced by various parties in the music industry.
Today, one of the main concerns is Napster, which gives everyone who
uses the software access to all the MP3 files on one another's
computers that they are willing to share. Napster's own servers compile
a large, constantly updated index of all the music available from its
users. Users simply type in the song title or name of the artist they are
looking for, and Napster generates a list of other users who already
have it. Clicking on one of the selections automatically copies the file
from one user's hard drive to the other's.

Many in the music industry believe programs like Napster will cause
music listeners to cease purchasing musical recordings. Indeed, a
recent New York Times article highlights the use of Napster by a
college student who downloaded 800 musical recordings from the
Internet. There are others, though, who believe that free access to
music via the Internet is a powerful marketing tool and that this new
form of distribution will help, not hurt, sales of musical recordings. The
development of this type of software also has ramifications for the
movie industry. Once this file sharing software is perfected and digital
delivery via the Internet becomes quicker, computer users may be able
to swap high-quality movie files in the same way, thus impacting film
studios, movie theaters, and video rental chains.

In this age of Napster, and other file sharing programs like Gnutella, the question arises as to how will record labels and musicians control the distribution of their music and will they be able to make a profit? The Recording Industry Association of America (RIAA) has undertaken the long-awaited Secure Digital Music Initiative which is working to develop an open, interoperable architecture and specification for digital music security. Once completed, purchasers of SDMI compliant music files and software will be able to play their music in SDMI compliant portable and home players. Until then, though, there are a multitude of file formats available on the Internet, most without the copyright protection that SDMI compliant files are projected to have.

In the music industry, as well as other industries we have examined, the Internet is purported to be able to balance the inequities faced by small entities. While it is true that smaller businesses have the flexibility to adapt quickly to changes in the marketplace, I am concerned about their ability to absorb losses that they may incur due to piracy. Additionally, in the wilderness of the Internet, how will small music labels be able to get their voices heard above the roar of the Big (soon to be) Four record labels?

To answer these questions and to provide us with excellent background on these issues we have a distinguished panel of witnesses. Ric Dube is a Senior Analyst and Editor with Webnoize, which focuses on the entertainment industry's relationship with the Internet; Tom Silverman, Founder and CEO of Tommy Boy Records, who is testifying on behalf of the RIAA; Peter Harter, Vice-President for Global Public Policy and Standards of Emusic.com., the Internet's leading retailer of licensed and authorized MP3 music files; and Chuck D, recording artist and founder of Rapstation.com which features free MP3 downloads, a television station and information for aspiring artists. I look forward to the testimony of our witnesses.

55

Statement of Congresswoman Bono
May 24, 2000
House Committee on Small Business
Digital Music Distribution Models

Mr. Chairman, on a number of levels I am deeply interested in the issue we will be discussing today, and I am certain that there are many throughout the country who share this interest and have been anticipating congressional action on this issue.

On the one hand, we have those who are interested in what is said in this room today as it could effect the future of copyright, the future of musicians and other performers , and have considerable impact on consumers. And on the other hand, there are those who are watching the debate on this issue to analyze what direction the digital music industry is going to move, and where the money is going to flow. I am here on this committee to represent my district, to represent the interests of small businesses across the country, and to represent the music community as a whole.

While many may feel that what is in the best interest of all those communities are mutually exclusive, I believe that in a world where technology moves so rapidly the solution to the issues in question today could be right around the corner.

As a Member of Congress who also studies these issues in the House Committee on Judiciary, I also wholeheartedly believe that the industry should be the one to find this solution. To open up the Digital Millennium Copyright Act for amendment to address the copyright infringement issues that have been brought to light could have widespread implications for the technology industry as a whole.

From the standpoint of the artist, I would like to see an environment where the artist can decide the best way to distribute their music. For the consumer, I believe that the music fans should be able to depend on the material that they are receiving. And for the record companies, I believe that there is a way that they can collect the return on the significant risk that is put forth in signing artists to their label.

It is my hope that today's hearing will bring all of those interests into perspective and give us direction as to how Congress and the internet industry should move on this issue.

Ric Dube
Analyst
Webnoize
179 Sidney St.
Cambridge MA 02139

(617) 768-0400
rdube@webnoize.com

Dr. Ric Dube is an analyst for **Webnoize**, the leading authority on the digital entertainment industry. Founded in 1994, Webnoize provides news coverage and analysis of the entertainment industry's developing relationship with the Internet, new media, cross-markets and emerging technologies. Webnoize reaches 75,000 music, film, broadcast, technology, telecommunication, consumer electronics, media, business and new media industry leaders.

An expert in research design, specializing in survey construction and data analysis, Dube taught mass media and communications at the University of Connecticut and University of Washington, and managed major research projects for the City of Seattle and RXL Pulitzer, a partnership between Pulitzer Inc., Morgan Murphy Broadcasting and The Rockey Company. For four years Dube was lead analyst at the Center for Social Science Computing and Research (CSSCR) in Seattle, an internationally active think tank.

Dube regularly speaks at entertainment and technology industry gatherings worldwide, and is a regular presence in print and broadcast media outlets, including the *Wall Street Journal*, *New York Times*, *Los Angeles Times*, *Rolling Stone* magazine, Reuters, CNN, MTV, CNET Radio, the *Chicago Tribune* and the *Boston Globe*.

A published author on the mechanics of persuasion, attitude change, and media credibility, Dube has a Ph.D. from the University of Washington.

Prepared Statement of Ric Dube
Analyst, Webnoize
Before the Subcommittee on Small Business, May 24, 2000

Mr. Chairman and members of the subcommittee, on behalf of Webnoize, thank you for inviting me to testify today at this very important hearing regarding the future of music on the Internet and small businesses.

I'm Ric Dube, an analyst with Webnoize and interim editor of the company's news publications. I've been on the Internet since 1991, an Internet industry professional since 1994, and I've always been a music fan and consumer.

Webnoize provides news coverage and analysis of the entertainment industry's relationship with the Internet, new media, cross-markets and emerging technologies. Our news reports reach well over 75.000 industry leaders in music, film. broadcasting, technology, telecommunication, consumer electronics, media and business.

We started Webnoize with what was at the time a bold premise: that the Internet represents the single most significant outcome of the post-Industrial Revolution, but does not represent a revolution itself -- it is an evolution. The Internet represents change, progress and opportunity.

Our news is published all day, every work day, from our offices in Cambridge, Massachusetts, at our web site. Each year in Los Angeles, we host the largest, most successful annual conference showcasing and discussing how new technologies affect the music industry.

We've always covered small businesses, because the Internet presents as much opportunity for them to flourish as it does to massive conglomerates. The problem for both is that taking advantage of the Internet to evolve a business requires understanding outside of the core competencies of many existing companies.

Someone from one of the subcommittee member's offices asked me yesterday whether large online retailers like Amazon.com were hurting privately-owned music retailers. Not yet. Internet sales of music are actually not all that impressive -- about 1% of all music sold is sold online, about the same in 1999 as in 1998.

It's true that traditional record stores have lost about 20% of their market share over the last ten years, but most of that ground has been lost to electronics superstores and department stores that sell CDs as a loss leader. If anything is hurting Mom & Pop record shops, its the growth of superstores and large music chains in the real world, not the virtual world.

But I did say not yet. The Internet will affect small retailers in the long run -- but not because Amazon.com sells CDs. It's because the Internet is so much more interesting than a convenient place to sell CDs.

Around the office we have an internal slogan -- one of many -- we say that "the Web is passe." The World Wide Web is just one manifestation of the Internet, an information network that can add functionality to any electronic device. There's a microwave oven in development by Samsung, a refrigerator by Frigidaire, and wireless telephones all over Europe and Asia. all of which offer Internet connectivity.

The Internet is not just a way to use a personal computer. Using the Internet to grow a business is not about putting up a dot-com site. For example, traditional music retailers like Virgin Megastores, HMV and the Trans World chains are planning ways to bring the Internet into their stores to provide more comprehensive services.

Imagine stepping up to a kiosk in a record store, browsing through a list of the top 40 hits of the day, selecting 12 of your favorites and having a CD of them created for you while you wait. With digital Internet connections, CD burners and laser printing, nothing ever need be out-of-stock or out-of-print.

This is my MP3 player. It weighs a couple of ounces and holds about two hours of digital music. I'm looking forward to a day when I can pop a device like this into a slot in a Tower Records kiosk at the airport to load it up with music -- an hour of songs I ask for specifically, and an hour of songs I have never heard yet it simply knows I'll enjoy.

We're quite a ways off from that for now. And it's unlikely that a small independent retailer would bother to participate in that sort of market opportunity. The opportunity for small retailers is to extend what has always been their core competency -- serving consumer niches.

We know that this is already working. According to a survey by the National Association of Recording Merchants, while Internet retail represents about 1% of chain store sales, they represent about 3% of sales at independent stores.

The natural course of the market is to limit the number of sellers, but it never lasts long because consumers grow frustrated when generalized services fail to meet individual needs -- and small businesses come in to fill the gap.

Small independent record labels serve the same function. They release the music that the major record companies don't. It's music that plays to a significantly smaller audience, but generally one that cares more about its music.

The Internet has been great for independent music. Web sites let small labels market their acts to audiences in ways TV and radio could never allow. Any band that wants to promote itself online can upload music and pictures to MP3.com, Riffage, GarageBand.com, or the Internet Underground Music Archive. MP3.com offers music by 67,000 artists, one or two of which actually make a living from the CDs they sell through the site.

The independent labels have led the charge to experiment with downloadable music. Giving away downloadable songs can be a great way to expose music that will not get airplay on the radio or on MTV. By doing that, indie labels are leading a very provocative experiment -- finding out whether giving away music online affects sales, and if so, in what direction.

You may have heard about Napster. Napster has been called by music executives the most insidious development on the Internet. Whether or not it is that, it is certainly one of the most ingenious.

Napster is not a web site per se, rather it is a software application that lets Internet users compare lists of MP3 music files, and make copies of them. Most of the files available using Napster are illegally reproduced copies of copyright protected music. Millions of songs are available through Napster, for free.

Napster is most popular with college students, who have high-bandwidth Internet connections in their dormitories, and can download music quickly. A Webnoize survey found that over 70% of students are using Napster at least monthly -- more than 19% are using it daily.

I met a young woman who complained to me about dorm life. She hated the food and the noise and her roommate. I asked her, "Why don't you move out?" And she said, "I don't know where I'd get my music."

In that same Webnoize study, 63% of students said they are listening to more music downloaded from the Internet than one year ago. 23% said they are spending significantly less time listening to CDs.

Is Napster killing the music industry? Well, it would be rash to assume that everytime someone downloads an illegal music file the recording industry has lost a sale. When music is free people will try a lot they wouldn't have otherwise. And while Napster may have enabled the worst climate for casual piracy ever, the music industry is growing. Total revenue is up, CD shipments are up. It's worth wondering whether free music and MP3 swapping have stimulated sales.

Or it's possible that sales and shipments would be up even higher, if it weren't for all of the Internet music piracy going on. We know that Napster is most popular with young people; the market share for music accounted for by consumers between the ages of 15-24 has dropped considerably over the last decade.

But they love Napster. We asked college students who use Napster whether they'd be willing to pay $15 per month to use it, and more than 58% said they would. It hints that it might be time for the recording industry to consider the possibility of letting people pay for music, not just by the song or by the album, but by the month.

Napster touts the size of its user base as its strength. They have about 10 million users. I don't know if any of them care about the Napster community. I think they like Napster because that's where the content is. Record companies have released very little of their music on the Internet. The entertainment industry is a supply/demand dynamic, and when supply fails to come through, demand creates its own supply.

It's a consumer version of the notion that small businesses fill the niche gaps left behind when there are too few sellers. New revenue models for music like digital distribution, subscription access, personalized radio, pay-per-view webcasts -- all are possible and for now there's nothing stopping independent labels or private retailers from getting in on them.

It won't be long before the most enterprising businesses on the Internet are run by the artists themselves. The Internet enables music distribution and programming that fans will pay for; artists that already have a following will leave the established music label system and strike out on their own.

I value companies like Napster because they have great ideas and they put them in action. Just as major labels watch to see which independent artists have wide commercial potential, they are also watching smart young companies to see which ideas to co-opt.

Thank you for the opportunity to testify this morning. I would be pleased to answer any questions you may have.

**Testimony of Tom Silverman
before the Small Business Committee May 24, 2000**

My name is Tom Silverman. I am CEO of Tommy Boy Records. I started my company twenty years ago because I had a vision for an independent record company that could create a haven for artists to explore their music on their own terms. I served on the Board of Directors of the American Federation of Independent Music (AFIM) for 13 years, a coalition of independent record companies as well as serving as one of the several independent members of the board of the Recording Industry Association of America (RIAA). While I may have a unique perspective in the industry overall, I am here today to talk about the particular issues important to small record labels like mine – the widespread illegal distribution of music on the Internet.

Without a doubt, the Internet provides a tremendous opportunity for many small businesses today, and especially small record labels such as Tommy Boy Records. Never before could a small company like Tommy Boy interact with its customers so well to the benefit of both. Through Tommy Boy's web site, www.tommyboy.com, customers can listen to portions of their favorite music and get a taste of some of the other music that appears on the Tommy Boy label. Someone who comes to the site to hear more from Everlast, one of Tommy Boy's most popular artists, may also become curious about the most recent offerings of De La Soul, another Tommy Boy artist. Thus, through the use of the Internet, Tommy Boy can not only build relationships with those who buy Tommy Boy's sound recordings, it can also build on those relationships by introducing those customers to other sound recordings they might purchase.

The greatest benefit the Internet provides to small companies is its ability to dramatically reduce the burdens of nationwide – even worldwide – distribution of products. Small record labels often form relationships with major record labels such as Warner Brothers or Universal to distribute compact discs nationally or worldwide. While we value access to the majors' distribution channels, the money paid for distribution cuts into the amount of money small record labels can spend on finding, developing, and marketing new artists. Through the Internet, however, small labels such as Tommy Boy can sell and distribute their artists' music without forming those distribution relationships. Whether by compact disc or digital audio file, Tommy Boy can sell its artists' music directly to the people who want to buy it. Indeed, worldwide distribution can be achieved simply by operating a Web site.

However, as easy as it is for Tommy Boy to distribute music over the Internet, it is even easier for Internet users to copy Tommy Boy's music and distribute it worldwide. A single copy of a song can be copied an unlimited number of times and distributed worldwide via the Internet without any degradation in quality. Those without respect for the copyright laws can distribute illegal copies of an Everlast song to thousands of Internet users, many of whom would otherwise pay Tommy Boy for a copy of that song. This illegal distribution costs not only Tommy Boy, but the artists to whom Tommy Boy pays royalties.

This is a very serious and widespread problem for us, involving more than simply a few bad apples who distribute music illegally. Unfortunately, the current culture of the Internet could be described as a culture of infringement. This culture of infringement is based on the notion that use of the Internet – because it is relatively new and exciting and makes copying and distribution easy, fast and cheap – somehow makes the copying and distribution of copyrighted material acceptable. A perfect example of this attitude would be the reaction of some people to the lawsuit files against Napster. A number of Internet users have expressed disappointment with this decision because it fails to embrace new technology. This attitude can only be described as a belief that Internet users have not only immunity for their copying but a right to distribute other people's creative work – which is the life's blood of my business. This belief in immunity is fostered by the anonymity of the Internet – people use aliases and user names so that their real "selves" aren't the ones doing the illegal copying. The result of this culture of infringement is that perfectly reasonable people who would never walk into a Tower Records and steal a compact disc because they believe that to be wrong are doing the same on the Internet when they seek out and download illegal copies of music from the Internet.

Programs like Napster – which allow Internet users to find illegal copies of songs and download them anonymously – are menacing to small record labels because they were designed to facilitate the culture of infringement. Napster is a business that just received $15 million in venture capital funding. They obviously are in this to make money. By providing access to every illegal MP3 file residing on the computer of every user connected to the Napster system, Napster acts as a supermarket for infringement. Because Napster has millions of users, the Napster network is vast and nearly every popular sound recording is available for download through the Napster service.

Perhaps even more insidiously, the Gnutella software provides a similar service – but runs without a central computer server. Thus, with Gnutella, there is no central place where the infringement occurs and no one target for a record label's antipiracy efforts.

This widespread illegal reproduction and distribution of music on the Internet threatens the very creation of music – a result ignored by those who make and distribute illegal copies supposedly for the "love" of music. The designer of the Gnutella program has been described as believing that "everything should be free." Indeed, the Gnutella program threatens to make all music free – thus eliminating the opportunity for recording artists and labels to earn a fair return on their creative and financial investments.

It takes considerable resources to produce, promote and distribute a recording properly. Small record labels such as mine must find new artists, fund the recordings (at a cost of $50,000 to $500,000,) market the recording, produce videos, fund advertising in media, implement a press and public relations strategy, distribute promotion copies, fund individual radio and video promotions, and incur retail placement charges. After all of this investment, less than 20% of the recordings Tommy Boy Records develops and promote will turn a profit, and we have a success average that is four times better than the major labels. It takes us 5 swings to get a hit and if we bat .200 in our releases, that's a great year. Here are some important statistics to consider. There were 38,857 albums released last year; 7,000 from the majors and 31, 857 from independents like me. Out of the total releases, only 233 sold over 250,000 units. Only 437 sold over 100,000 units. So less than 1% of all releases last year were profitable. That kind of investment needs to be protected and cannot be balanced against a threat of digital piracy that would make the risks so high so as to be untenable. There is very little point in spending the time, talent and money necessary to find, develop and promote new artists when that investment cannot be recovered in the form of sales to customers. A reduced incentive to create new music means that less new music is created, a consequence that not even the most blatant infringers want.

The reduced incentive I am discussing is not theoretical or speculative, but is here right now. The widespread infringement of copyrights through FreeNet, Napster, Gnutella, and other services and programs is a deterrent to distributing music legally on the Internet. One of the reasons Tommy Boy does not allow its customers to download its artists' music as an alternative to purchasing a compact disc is that we fear that those downloaded copies will be copied and distributed without further payment. Although Tommy Boy views Internet distribution of music as an incredible opportunity to reach new fans and new customers, that opportunity must be weighed against the loss of compensation that will occur due to illegal copying and distribution. Moreover, small record labels such as Tommy Boy simply do not have the resources to pursue legal actions against the multitude of infringers out there, thus making the small record labels particularly ripe targets for Internet pirates. As long as people are using Gnutella, FreeNet, Napster, the risk of lost compensation is too high for Tommy Boy to offer its artists' music for sale directly through the Internet.

But the damages caused by the widespread infringement facilitated by Napster, Gnutella, and FreeNet transcend the financial loss to record labels such as Tommy Boy. These damages reach the artist as well. Artists such as my friend and fellow witness Chuck D are not compensated unless their own property is respected on the Internet. Every lost sale is a lost royalty. More importantly, creative control is put at risk by Napster and Gnutella. Before the band Metallica's most recent CD ever was released to the public, several versions – unfinished and unpolished – were available for unlimited and worldwide distribution over Napster. These versions were not the final form of

Metallica's creative vision, and thus not the ultimate expression of their music. And of course, a musician's expression is the very foundation of his music.

In conclusion, small companies who provide creative content on the Internet, and small record labels especially, are being hurt by the widespread infringement of copyrights on the Internet. Not only are small labels losing money every time a user downloads a copy of a recording by an artist like Everlast from Napster, but we are effectively being prevented from pursuing the Internet as an option for distributing our artist's music. The deterrence caused by the widespread distribution of illegal copies – fostered by the culture of infringement – denies the small record labels from using the newest and best way to reach out to customers and fans and connecting them to the new and exciting music we produce.

I would like to thank you again for the opportunity to speak and will gladly answer any questions you might have.

Statement of

Peter Harter

Vice President Global Public Policy and Standards

EMusic.com, Inc.

Redwood City, CA

on

Online Music: Will Small Music Labels and Entrepreneurs Prosper in the Internet Age?

Before the

House Small Business Committee

United State House of Representatives

10:00am

24 May 2000

I.   Introduction.

Mr. Chairman, distinguished members of the Committee, good morning. My name is Peter F. Harter, and I would like to thank you for inviting me here today to testify before the Committee. You have invited me to acquaint Members of the Committee with the ways in which the Internet is already changing, and will continue to change, the channels of distribution for musical recordings. In addition, I will describe how small businesses and aspiring entrepreneurs can take advantage of new technologies to reduce barriers to entry from established competitors by reaching larger listening audiences. First, let me tell you about a small business selling music on the Internet.

II.   EMusic.com, Inc.

I am here in my capacity as Vice President for Global Public Policy and Standards of EMusic.com Inc. As one of the largest Internet sellers of digitally formatted music, EMusic.com is at the forefront of the newly emerging market for downloadable digital media products. This new market and the technology on which it is based have the potential to alter fundamentally the way in which music is distributed and consumed. Greater efficiencies in distribution, expanded consumer choice, and ease of access will result in lower prices, better products, and a larger overall market. This will benefit everyone -- consumers, artists and the entertainment industry.

EMusic was founded in January 1998 by Gene Hoffman and Bob Kohn, two executives from Pretty Good Privacy (PGP), with decades of combined experience in Internet start ups, software firms, security, and music licensing. Formerly known as GoodNoise Corp., EMusic has been publicly traded since May 1998 and can be found today on NASDAQ under the symbol "EMUS." EMusic has established itself at the forefront of how new music will be discovered, delivered and enjoyed. In addition to having the Internet's largest catalog of downloadable MP3 music available for purchase, EMusic operates one of the Web's most popular families of music-oriented Web sites -- including RollingStone.com, EMusic.com, DownBeatJazz.com, and IUMA. The company is based in Redwood City, California, with regional offices in Chicago, Los Angeles, New York and Nashville.

EMusic is the Web's leading site for sampling and purchasing music in the MP3 format, which has become the standard in the digital distribution of music. Through direct relationships with leading artists and exclusive licensing agreements with over 650 independent record labels, EMusic.com offers music fans an expanding collection of more than 100,000 tracks for purchase -- individual tracks for 99 cents each or entire downloadable albums for $8.99. EMusic.com features top artists in all popular musical genres, such as Alternative (Bush, Kid Rock, They Might Be Giants, Frank Black), Punk (Blink-182, The Offspring, Pennywise), Jazz (Duke Ellington, Dizzy Gillespie, Louis Armstrong, Concord Records), Blues (John Lee Hooker, B.B. King, Buddy Guy), Hip Hop (Kool Keith, The Coup), Country (Willie Nelson, Merle Haggard, Patsy Cline), Rock (Phish, Goo Goo Dolls, David Crosby), World (Nusrat Fateh Ali Kahn, Lee "Scratch" Perry) and Vintage Pop (Liza Minnelli, Eartha Kitt, Judy Garland).

To give you an idea of how fast the downloadable music industry is growing, the company has now sold over 1 million songs in the popular MP3 format since its launch. We have music from all genres and are aggressively acquiring the exclusive rights to digitally distribute the music from independent labels, artists and back catalogs. We have focused our digital distribution efforts on independent labels, artists and backcatalogs in order to level the promotion, marketing and distribution playing field for such participants in the music industry. Before the Internet, artists and independent labels were always at a disadvantage with regard to the power of the five major record labels. With open standards like the MP3 file format, Internet distribution and promotion firms like EMusic can help labels and artists reach a world-wide audience of consumers much more effectively than they could on their own. (To further explain MP3 technology, I have included a primer as an appendix to my written testimony.)

III.   Disintermediation.

For several years now the Internet economy has brought change. From buying airplane tickets online directly from the airline, to engaging in an auction, to buying music directly from the artist, the Internet has provided for new channels of distribution, marketing, and consumer awareness. The distributed nature of the Internet and the efficiencies inherent to computer based communications produce a new way for people to find great things that they did not even know they needed! In fact, many argue that the Internet actually reintermediates people and commerce. By taking out the middlemen, consumers gain more control over what is made available and how. Despite the moves by Old Economy firms to strap their old business models on to the Internet, consumers speak with their mouse clicks. Consumers often demonstrate how they want to conduct themselves on the Internet. Just take a look at how popular sites like Napster have become. Putting aside the controversy surrounding Napster for a moment, one can't help but acknowledge how rapidly Napster has built a huge base of users. By enabling users to swap music via the Internet Napster has enabled people to do something in cyberspace that they already do in physical space but in a new and strikingly efficient way. By reintermediating users Napster has in effect become a new sort of middleman. Users are in a more direct relation to one another. There are fewer middlemen than in the traditional retail experience.

Disintermediation impacts the artist in ways that are positive. Traditionally artists rely on the major labels for recording, distribution and marketing of their work. This has not changed in decades. Even the last major technological changes that occurred in the music industry -- the move from vinyl to CD's -- didn't change the nature of that relationship. Those technological changes were still controlled by the labels. The Internet, however, is controlled by no one person, entity or government. And as a result the Internet is taking the music industry in directions that the traditional forces may not understand, appreciate or like.

Indeed, with the emergence of the Internet the major labels, for the first time since their businesses were founded, have limited and diminishing control over the recording, distribution and marketing process. Literally anyone can now record, distribute and market music they create. Nothing will alter this progression. By its very nature the Internet is a disruptive technology force. It is not a place or a company – if anything it is a state of being. Plainly the Internet does not exist unless two or more computer networks are interconnected using the open standards of TCP/IP to transport data from one system to another, from one computer to another. Existing record companies must develop and implement business models that compliment these changes or they will be bypassed in the rapidly changing music industry. I think some of the majors are waking up to this reality – that is why one can read in the newspapers that the majors may settle their lawsuit against MP3.com by doing a business deal focused on subscriptions for their music.

IV.   Reintermediation.

A great example of reintermediation by a legitimate business is IUMA. The Internet Underground Music Archive (IUMA) was one of the first ever commercial sites on the Internet. EMusic bought IUMA last year to diversify our business so that it included the important function of helping amateur artists gain notoriety so that they would have a better opportunity to be discovered and go commercial. IUMA does not focus on selling its artist's music to consumers like EMusic. Instead, IUMA is a business to business (B2B) model; they provide the infrastructure and tools for artists to connect with other artists and most importantly to connect with labels, managers, and promoters. Artists build their own website in IUMA and IUMA analyzes their content and talent and fan base, compare it with other bands and other market data to provide a comprehensive database that managers, promoters, and labels use to evaluate new talent. Before the Internet artists had to cut their own tape or press their own CD and then walk it around to countless clubs and individuals before getting access to someone at a label. Sometimes an artist can be discovered at a live performance but that is much more random than the analytical engines of IUMA. IUMA does not replace the existing role for the talent in labels who do the A&R work – the development and management of an artist and their repertoire. Instead, IUMA enables both the artist and the label personnel to do their jobs more effectively with better information.

V. Competition: Competing with Free Music

As a general matter, the less regulation, the better, but there are areas in which the law must set structure to enable progress. That legal architecture should support innovation, not obstruct it. If the law is at cross-purposes to technological progress, the law will be ineffective and technological and economic progress will be impeded. However, where the existing law is not being enforced or obeyed then equally negative results will occur. The Internet economy is more dependent on legal architecture than most are willing to admit. Despite the glut of rhetoric about how the Internet can't be regulated and how Silicon Valley relishes its independence from Washington, the software and music industries, for example, would not exist at all without regulation. Copyright law is the regulation that enables these industries to exist, to grow, and to gather revenue. But copyright law is not absolute. It is only a temporary monopoly granted for specific reasons to achieve specific public good purposes. Thomas Jefferson's vision of copyright is instructive. He cast copyright law as an incentive for citizens of an agrarian economy to invest their intellectual capacity in ways that advanced the sciences and the arts. Commerce and the industrial economy boomed for two centuries.

This ancient law has also enabled the information economy to appear and explode in size. But as I said earlier there are limits to copyright law; many agree that some regulation may impede business, innovation, and competition. It is no surprise that incumbent industries and business models lobby lawmakers to protect their existing way of doing business from new forms of competition that arise from technology. Congress has a very important role in striking a balance here between updating law as needed to continue protecting legitimate interests in copyright and preventing existing business models from leveraging the law to disadvantage innovation and competition. As many of you know these issues are of much discussion lately in Washington, DC, with regard to the Microsoft case. While that matter is very interesting and important there are many other examples that require the attention of Congress. Otherwise small businesses may suffer.

First, when Congress passed the Digital Millenium Copyright Act (DMCA) over a year ago it instructed the Copyright Office and the Commerce Department to produce a report on the issue of restricting research in the area of circumventing copyright protection measures and technologies. This is a classic case of catch 22. If one cannot legally hack protection schemes how does one know if they are really that strong? Legitimate research into encryption is necessary for the advancement of the sciences and the arts. And by its nature it is a form of human expression protected by the First Amendment. Unfortunately, this report has not been completed and is severely behind schedule. EMusic has provided comments to the Copyright Office and the Department of Commerce. Despite our best efforts as a small business I am concerned that this yet to be produced report may be delayed so that it does not upset the established interests of the traditional copyright community. That community includes the major record labels. It is an election year and no one wants to upset their friends or choose sides. This Administration has friends in both Hollywood and Silicon Valley. Delaying real, transparent debate of this issue will only disadvantage small businesses and play into the hands of larger, more established firms who better understand the nuances of policy making. Small high tech firms do not often lobby or understand the policy making process. In their absence larger firms gain ground. I strongly encourage this Committee to look into this matter further.

The second example concerns Napster. Napster is a small business in San Mateo, California. They are in Silicon Valley but they are not a technology company. In my opinion, they are not an innovator either. Briefly, Napster enables consumers to find music provided online by other individuals. It is a massive music sharing system fueled by a central database and directory operated by Napster. Many artists, record labels and music publishers are suing Napster for copyright infringement. While the courts and parties involved are trying to work out the issues involved, there is one issue that should be of concern to Congress: Will Napster cause Congress to reopen the DMCA? Many carefully crafted compromises make up the delicate balances achieved in the DMCA. One of those compromises is OSP liability. Internet and online service providers do not want to impede the flow of data through their networks. They do not want to play the role of big brother and monitor all traffic. However, they do work within some limits. The DMCA's notice and take down provisions exemplify such limits. Napster has tried to dress itself as a mere ISP so that it can take advantage of the defenses in the DMCA. The courts are so far unconvinced by Napster on this point. One may suggest that Napster admit that it really is a PSP – a piracy service provider. It would be interesting to see Napster lobby themselves into copyright law. Seriously, I am one of the last people in the industry to be in favor of using copyright law to stop a new business model. But Napster's model, as wildly popular as it is with consumers, threatens to upset the DMCA. In this case the balance for Congress to strike may be against a small business in favor of the established regulatory architecture. Congress must be careful not to harm the underlying technology Napster exploits; file sharing technology has been around for a very long time on the Internet and is an essential part of the Internet's architecture. But just as Congress deftly dealt with the difficult issue of caching and proxying and the copyright of reproduction, Congress can work out an effective public policy that deals with file sharing business models, and if need be, with the technologies themselves perhaps. Again, I must emphasize that this area of law and technology is complicated and not without controversy. There are no easy answers and government should not act rashly. But Congress should not sit idly by; examination and discussion are necessary.

VI.   Conclusions:

Companies that seek to exploit artists work for commercial profit -- without compensating the artists -- will end up forcing increased regulatory oversight that may stifle innovation and result in greater restrictions on consumers access to artists work. The DCMA established the framework we need to keep innovative technology coming to the marketplace while still fairly compensating artists. As a leader in pioneering the online digital music revolution, EMusic believes that for the online music industry to continue to grow, businesses must work within the established framework laid out by DCMA. This includes new, small businesses like Napster. Whether start ups like it or not they cannot ignore the policy making process. Copyright law and many others shape the environment in which businesses operate. It is one thing to run a business idea out of college dorm room; it is entirely another to grow that idea into a commercial business with investors, employees, shareholders and customers. The Small Business Committee may wish to find a way to specifically engage the start up community from around the country in a conversation about the policy making process. This would be a useful way to build a relationship between high tech and government; the alternative is naked regulation based on insufficient input from the small business community.

While there has recently been widespread media coverage of sites offering "free" or "shared" music online, the underlying reality is much different. Consumers may not be paying directly for music, but remember these sites are in fact in business and are currently -- or will be -- seeking to profit from traffic to these sites. We all remember the old adage "if it seems like it's too good to be true it probably is" well that still applies. What consumers may believe is free today, may end up depriving future generations of easy access to music. We, at EMusic, would like to see businesses continue to deliver new technology and music to consumers, but we also would like to see them do it in a way that respects artists rights and is consistent with DCMA. EMusic is proud to be in the forefront of that approach.

The alternative is increased litigation, increased regulation, and increased hassles and costs for music lovers. And in the end no one benefits from that.

Appendix I

MP3: a primer

In 1999, the term "MP3" replaced "sex" as the most popular term inputted into search engines over the world. The reason was simple: MP3 is the most flexible and user-friendly music format around.

MP3, which stands for "MPEG1 Layer 3", is a compression format that enables CD-quality music to easily be transferred across the Internet. Best yet, MP3 is an open standard, meaning anyone can use it. It's revolutionizing the way people listen to music.

This guide to MP3 will (hopefully) provide any MP3 novice with the tools and knowledge to take advantage of this new technology.

1. Getting Started

The first step in joining the MP3 revolution is getting a player for your PC. There are dozens of free MP3 players available for download over the Internet and it's likely there's already one on your hard-drive now. If you're not sure whether you have a player, we recommend downloading **Error! Bookmark not defined.** for Windows 95/98, a wonderful and easy to use MP3 player. It is available for free at http://www.freeamp.com.
If you use Macintosh, try downloading a **Error! Bookmark not defined.**, an MP3 player for Macintosh. It is available at http://www.macast.com. Or you can choose one from our full list of recommended playersfor more choices (see below)

2. Downloading Music

To download your first MP3, go to http://www.emusic.com/music/free/html and choose a free track, courtesy of Emusic.
How long it takes to download will depend on the speed of your computer and modem. If you're on a T1 or DSL line, it often only take seconds to download.

You can also check out the **Error! Bookmark not defined.** (www.IUMA.com) for free MP3s from artists that are yet to be "discovered."

3. Playing Your Songs

Now, simply start up your MP3 player and open the file by pressing the "file" option on your player. Your player may have already opened the file automatically.

At this point, you should be listening to quality music on your computer. Now you're left with a number of options for what you want to do with your new MP3 file. You can **Error! Bookmark not defined.** for playback on an ordinary CD player. You can even **Error! Bookmark not defined.**.

As you can see, you can do just about anything with MP3. You can now enjoy the future of music!

<u>Additional Information: Hardware and Software</u>

I.   MP3 players for your computer

There are plenty of MP3 players that can be downloaded for free. Each one has its own benefits. Here's a rundown of some of the best-known players:

- Freeamp (http://www.freeamp.com) has great sound and an easy-to-use interface. Like a standard CD player, it has a shuffle function that will let you play songs you have downloaded at random. The interface is small and non-intrusive. Since it's free, it doesn't constantly advertise for upgrades like some of the other players.

- RealNetworks' RealJukebox (http://www.real.com/jukebox/index.html) is easily one of the most well-known software products in the world. In addition to MP3, it also plays RealAudio files and other formats. RealNetworks enjoys 80 percent of the market share when it comes to PC audio players. Like many players, it comes in both a free version and a pay version with added features.

- Winamp (http://www.winamp.com) is famous for its wide variety of "skins." A "skin" is basically a new look or interface for a software product. This product has plenty of them. A simple Internet search will turn up hundreds (if not thousands) of free skins you can download to suit even the strangest of tastes. To see a site specifically devoted to providing new WinAmp looks, go to http://www.winamp-skins.com.

- Musicmatch Jukebox (http://www.musicmatch) is an incredibly versatile product that enables you to record, download and convert digital audio. It also features an AutoDJ to create custom playlists. When you start putting your MP3 files on compact disc, you may want to use this program (but we'll delve more into that a little later.)

- Sonique (http://www.sonique.com) is one of the most visually stunning audio players. It comes equipped with all the features you'd expect from a media application, along with a playlist editor, 20-band graphic equalizer and standard CD-player-like controls.

- SoundJam MP (http://www.soundjam.com) Macintosh users, take notice. This is the first MP3 player and encoder for the Macintosh. It also enables you to set up playlists and convert other audio files you might have on your Macintosh into MP3s.

- MACAST (http://www.macast.net) is a leading Macintosh MP3 player that features a variety of "skins" (i.e., different user interfaces), an auto-sleep function, 10-band equalizer and more.

- Xmms (http://www.xmms.org) Another player for those using an operating system other than your standard Windows OS, this is WinAmp for X Windows, under the Unix operating system.

- SoundPlay (http://www.xs4all.nl/~marcone/soundplay.html) The only product we know of that can play MP3 files backwards! It also lets you mix files or fade out of one and into another. It works with the BeOS operating system, an alternative to both the Windows and Macintosh operating systems.

II.   Hardware options

There are a number of MP3 players available on the market that will enable you to listen to MP3s while jogging, driving or just sitting at home.

You can certainly play MP3s on your home stereo. The most common way of doing this is by recording the music to a blank compact disc for playback on an ordinary CD player (see below). This takes a little know-how and a do-it-yourself attitude, but it's a lot of fun. You can also record the music to CD multiple times, creating a number of different CDs.

III.   Converting MP3s to CDs

Many aren't aware that MP3 files can almost instantly be converted and recorded to compact disc.

In order to do this, you just need some free software. Using MusicMatch Jukebox (http://www.musicmatch.com), for instance, you simply go under "file" in the options menu. Then choose "convert." From this point on, you just choose the MP3 files you want converted into WAV files and the folders you want these new WAV files saved to.

Then, go into Adaptec Easy CD Creator (or whatever software you use to burn compact discs) to burn the WAV files onto a CD.

Note that MusicMatch can be downloaded for free, but promises better sound quality if you pay $29.99 for an upgrade. In terms of converting MP3s you've downloaded from EMusic.com, however, you shouldn't notice any difference in the quality of sound between the pay and free versions of MusicMatch.

The free version of MusicMatch, by the way, can be downloaded at the company's web site at http://www.musicmatch.com.

Other softwares:

- SonicFoundry's Siren Jukebox, available in an Xpress version for free or in a $39.95 that features CD writing capability, is just one product that will let you select a group of MP3 files and, in one fell swoop, write them all to a blank CD for playback on an ordinary stereo. Although SonicFoundry's software comes bundled with many CD-writers for free, the best version of the software is available at their web site, www.sonicfoundry.com.

- MusicMatch Jukebox 5.0 is available in a free format that lets you record your MP3 music to CD. A free download at www.musicmatch.com, the Jukebox is also available in a pay version that has more features.

- Another pay product that can enable you to instantly record MP3 music to a CD-R for playback on a conventional CD player is the Adaptec SoundStream, available from www.adaptec.com for $49. Adaptec, maker of the Easy CD Creator, is known for producing excellent CD burning software.

IV.   Portable Players

For many, the ultimate MP3 experience comes from listening to the files on a portable player. These players are the hottest devices to hit the music market since the original WalkMan.

They deliver CD-quality sound in a tiny, tiny size. You could download an album worth of music from EMusic.com and, in addition to playing it on your PC, quickly upload it into a portable player to take it on the road with you. The players are so small that they easily fit into your pocket.

And of course, if you have a portable compact disc player, you can also listen to MP3s on that device. All you need to do is **Error! Bookmark not defined.**

House Committee on Small Business

"Online Music: Will Small Music Labels And Entrepreneurs Prosper In The Internet Age?"

May 24, 2000

Presented byChuck D.
Founder, Rapstation.com

I would like to say I admire the comments and facts and figures and respect everything that Mr. Dube and Mr. Harter have said about their business models, so I am not going to repeat many of the same things that they said; and in all due respect to Tommy Silverman, who I have worked with before, a great guy, and he also has a fantastic business model as an independent record company, all due respect; but the major corporations have caused the conditions that made it difficult for independent companies and artistry to compete in the game of music.

We at Rapstation.com, and me personally, have been involved in downloadable distribution for about 5 years as a saving grace for my artistry, and have used downloadable digital distribution to microfocus upon a niche of rap music that I have been involved with. It has helped build a world community through communication, cultural exchange, in 40 countries I deal with on a regular -- and I take advantage of rap's worldwide experience, and I just think the corporate imbalances of the images making rap music and hip hop, like jail, gang banging, and drug culture is balanced out with everybody participating into the reflecting imagery.

At Rapstation.com I also engage with thousands of artists to equally market their music without complaint because they control and own their own destiny. So I choose artistry over industry any day of the week.

Also, we also have to realize technology trumps technology's every time. The 20th century tree that was so fruitful, you might not be able to pick from so easily. Napster or downloadable distribution, like we would call it, file sharing, is leading a one million MP3 march. It trades music like baseball cards, and digital distribution and file sharing is like those asteroids that wiped out all the dinosaurs. And in this case the dinosaurs are the big four, Sony, BMG, Time Warner and Universal.

Now these companies, which will soon probably be three any week now, have always prided themselves in the excitement of the music industry and the fans. Well, Napster and downloadable distribution is the biggest excitement since disco rap and the Beatles. It is like new radio. And it is not just free music, but it is a watchdog method for one site industrial rip-off. The chickens have finally come home to roost.

I think if people look at the artificial price hiking of CDs, something they made for as little as 80 cents and then charged the consumers, in cahoots with retail, for as high as $17, that has never been explained to the public up until recently. They have taken advantage of the artist and the public, squeezing out the small entrepreneur with a lawyer-accountant mentality, and now the industry is now begging government for this illusion for their inconvenience.

The Federal Trade Commission also found out the record companies were actually hiking their prices on the public; and they said, okay, how do you feel as an artist?

First of all, I think the system had to be eradicated for everybody to participate and start from scratch. For the first time you have the consumer in the audience participating in the music business. And how do we get paid? Well, technology will be there again, but the select process and the dominance will be eradicated, and now things will truly be shared. A business model will come up out of this in the new century. It won't destroy the old companies, but it will reconfigure their ways.

Piracy, well, the talk of the label 's bottom line is always the case, and that is why they are screaming. To protect artists, that is some BS.

82

They come up with these promotional copies and they press up 5,000 or 10,000 and, in many of the cases they go to waste. And the downloadable distribution, you have something that is called on demand, and I know that there is an artist graveyard out there of artists, especially black artists, back since Bessie Smith in 1923, that have much more complaints than downloadable distribution. Their complaints happen to be with the one-sided contracts.

I have signed a contract that said worldwide rights, and they couldn't sell the records in Africa, South America or Asia. So why am I signing something that says worldwide rights?

Then they say, well, the world and the universe. So that means if I get to Venus, they got the right to sell my records? So they want to control cyberspace, too, without knowing what it is.

I would bet, because of the corporate quagmire, more than 50 percent of all artistry is just stuck on shelves or never comes out in the public anyway. So I think it is very imperative for artists to adapt to the technology, to try to avoid this one-sided monopoly, because I do think it is collusion, for companies now have to share the marketplace; and I look forward to one million artists and one million labels all on the Internet.

Now, RIAA, they only answer to people who are usually former lawyers and accountants who have assumed executive jobs, taking in as high as eight-figure salaries. I have never seen eight figures, but to look at a company's president who is using stockholders' money and pulling in $18 million for a year, when he gets fired, as an artist I have got a beef. So, you know, if it ain't about the artist, the industry damn sure ain't caring about the fans either, because why would they charge them $17 for something that they make for 79 cents? So I think this organizes and creates a new infrastructure.

New templates will be created. Yes, 95 percent of all music will be free, but it has always been 5 percent that has driven it. And now it is a global entertainment business. And I think the biggest beef, just like Mr. Harter said, is that now the entertainment business -- and we are not just talking records companies, we are talking movie industry and television -- the entertainment business is morphing into the "entertain-net" business. And now you have technology companies that will actually push the button, as opposed to these ex-lawyers and accountants that just happen to push pencils and somehow fall into a 9 million a year salary there. I still don't know what they got paid for.

So do I think it will hurt actual sales? Nope. They said the same thing back in 1967 with FM radio. They said the same thing with the advent of the cassette recorder. The same beefs popped up. People can tape, but they will still go to Blockbuster. If they can get HBO and Cinemax and Showtime and they can tape on their VCR, what makes them go to Blockbuster? Blockbuster depends on them people bringing back their videos 8 days late. That is how they make their money.

So these companies will still be around. I think the laziness of the American public will also keep the entertainment or the "entertain-net" business at an all-time high. And this new digital distribution will be exposure, and now, truly, we have global exposure.

I am here testifying in the United States of America in front of Congress, but the Island of Dominica has nothing to do with this government and, therefore, they will get the music, too, and then all of a sudden you will have Asia, Africa and South America able to get the music.

So I think it is imperative now that the artists also understand that they can go to these places and become business people of their own or set up their own business teams instead of being locked outside the door because they don't happen to be in the offices of New York, LA Or Nashville. So now the hands are all in the pot together. There are a million hands in the pot, and that is why you hear a lot of screaming.

I am not screaming. I had ties with Universal, Universal, Edgar B and the Universal Crew. And I had a lawyer tell me, well, Chuck, you sold millions of records here, but you will never see a dime because you owe us. And I said, like hell I do.

So do you think I care about them? No. I am doing better in the digital system selling 10 copies, even if 100 people or 1,000 or 1,000,000 people get my music for free. If I know 1,000 that are coming my way, I will deal with that as opposed to somebody being shady.

84

Home
Recording
Rights
Coalition

The Honorable James Talent, Chairman
The Honorable Nydia Velazquez, Ranking Member
Small Business Committee
U.S. House of Representatives
Washington, DC 20515

STATEMENT OF THE HOME RECORDING RIGHTS COALITION
CONCERNING THE INTERNET AND THE INDEPENDENT MUSIC MARKET

The Home Recording Rights Coalition ("HRRC")[1] submits this summary statement for the hearing of the House Committee on Small Business concerning the impact of the Internet upon independent labels and retailers of recorded music.[2] Specifically, HRRC applauds Congress for wielding a light and balanced hand in regulating the Internet. This approach has allowed new ideas to incubate into compelling new business models. HRRC believes that the future success of the Internet is dependent upon continued Congressional restraint. We therefore express our opposition to the amendments to the Digital Millennium Copyright Act of 1998 proposed by the Progressive Policy Institute ("PPI") as premature, invasive of consumer interests, and ill-advised.

Congress Has Fueled the Technology Revolution Without Regulation

Independent musicians and record labels long have relied on alternative methods for exposing their music to potential new fans, from college radio airplay to encouraging the recording and swapping of consumer-made tapes. Internet services, like all digital technology, offer songwriters, recording artists, record labels and retailers unprecedented opportunities to build and market to the avid consumer fan base. Congress has played a key role in stimulating the growth of these new business models by wisely declining to over-regulate the Internet; and, whenever regulation was necessary, by enacting legislation that safeguarded the public interest in the availability and personal uses of copyrighted works. This hands-off approach has enabled entrepreneurs to unleash the genius of free enterprise to create new ways of exposing and selling recorded music online.

---

[1] The Home Recording Rights Coalition was formed in October, 1981, after the U.S. Court of Appeals for the Ninth Circuit held that the marketing of video recording products to consumers was a violation of U.S. copyright law. Although this decision was reversed by the Supreme Court in 1984, attempts by intellectual property owners to constrain the responsible exercise of consumer choice and discretion continue to this day.

[2] HRRC intends to submit a more complete written statement after the hearing for inclusion in the record.

A coalition of consumers, retailers, manufacturers and servicers of video and audio recording products.
P.O. Box 14267 • Washington DC 20044-4267 • 202-628-9212 • 800-282-8273
info@hrrc.org   www.hrrc.org

85

Two past examples of Congressional restraint are particularly instructive. First, despite calls for stricter copyright infringement standards by motion picture and recording companies throughout the 1980's and 1990's, Congress refused to enact legislation that would reverse or weaken the legal standard articulated by the Supreme Court in the 1984 "Betamax" case -- that manufacturers should not be liable for infringement by users of technologies that are capable of substantial noninfringing uses.[3] Second, when enacting copyright legislation affecting the rights of consumers, such as the Audio Home Recording Act of 1992 or the Digital Millennium Copyright Act of 1998, Congress has sought to carefully balance effective protection for copyright owners with the consumer's right to use technology for personal noncommercial purposes.

HRRC submits that it would be unwise for Congress to act precipitously, while these new music markets are still in their infancy, so as to restrict traditional consumer personal use rights, or to constrain new technological applications.

PPI's Proposals Threaten Existing Legal Principles and Business Practices, Where Neither Need Nor Benefit Has Been Shown.

In accordance with its recently updated core principles (attached hereto), HRRC wishes to make the following summary points:

1.   *Fair Use remains vital to consumer welfare in the digital age. Consumers should continue to be able to engage in time-shifting, place-shifting, and other private, noncommercial rendering of lawfully obtained music and video content.*

Only about one year ago, the recording industry filed suit to enjoin the sale of personal digital recorders for MP3 music, and lost. In Recording Industry Association of America v. Diamond Multimedia,[4] the Ninth Circuit Court of Appeals reaffirmed that traditional fair use principles must be flexibly applied to new digital personal recording devices. That court held that, like video time-shifting involved in the Betamax case, consumer "space-shift" recording of music from compact discs (or downloaded from the Internet) to computer hard drives, and from those hard drives to portable MP3 players, constituted a fair use that is wholly permissible under current copyright law.

While some clamored at that time for legislation to "solve" the portable device "problem," a better marketplace solution has emerged. Over the past year, recording companies recognized that it is preferable to work cooperatively with technology companies to embrace, not stifle, the technology market for downloadable music files and devices to record and play them. HRRC suggests here that Congress again should refrain from enacting new regulation, and should let the marketplace work.

---

3   Sony Corp. of America v. Universal City Studios, Inc., 464 U.S. 417, 421, 435 n.17, 439 (1984).

4   29 F. Supp. 624 (CD Cal. 1998), *affd*, 180 F.3d 1072 (9th Cir. 1999).

2.   *Products and services with substantial non-infringing uses, including those that enable fair use activities by consumers, should continue to be legal.*

A&M Records v. Napster, Inc. recasts in a new technological context the same fundamental policy issues addressed in the Betamax case of when or whether a manufacturer of a system with noninfringing uses can be held accountable for infringing acts committed by the system's users. Faced with the leading-edge "piracy tool" of the time -- the home videocassette recorder -- the Supreme Court in 1984 enunciated a flexible and durable standard, summarized above in this HRRC core principle, that balanced the rights of copyright owners and the public interests. One could not have predicted in 1984 the impact of the VCR on the video market. In hindsight, it would clearly have been a mistake to have outlawed the VCR, since by banning the technology the courts and Congress would also have outlawed the home video rental and sales markets. It similarly would be a mistake today to outlaw new music technologies that can satisfy the Betamax test for contributory infringement.

Some noninfringing uses exist for Napster. As one example, up-and-coming and platinum-selling artists have stated publicly that they do not oppose Napster or, more generally, the noncommercial exchange of their music over the Internet.[5] Other uses may be found by the courts to be fair use. Whether Napster can factually prove its claim that these are "substantial" noninfringing uses is an issue for the courts, not Congress. At this stage, long before any decision on the merits, it is premature for PPI to propose changing existing laws before the legal process has had a chance to work. The PPI paper is a solution in search of a problem.

3.   *Home recording practices have nothing to do with commercial retransmission of signals, unauthorized commercial reproduction of content, or other acts of "piracy." Home recording and piracy should not be confused.*

A fundamental flaw in the PPI paper is that it ignores this clear distinction between personal consumer behavior and commercial piracy. Consumers recording music to their hard drives are not "pirates." Kids introducing their online friends to new music are not "pirates." Congress long has known how to address willful commercial copyright infringement through the Copyright Act, and only recently has clarified the definition of and amplified the penalties for such commercial misconduct. By contrast, for more than 20 years Congress has declined to deem personal music uses as "piracy," and there is no reason to do so now.

4.   *Any technical constraints imposed on products or consumers by law, license or regulation should be narrowly tailored and construed, should not hinder*

---

[5]   HRRC notes, similarly, in the Betamax case, independent television producers such as Fred Rogers (known to millions of children as "Mister Rogers") testified that he had no objection to the VCR and, indeed, that he favored technologies that gave children and parents greater control over their viewing experience. See http://www.hrrc.org/mrrogers.html

87

technological innovation, and may be justified only to the extent that they foster the availability of content to consumers.

The proposals offered by the PPI would unjustifiably constrain products and business processes now "in beta" on the Internet. First, it is truly remarkable that PPI proposes the collection and verification of personal information -- a direct incursion upon personal privacy interests -- as a prerequisite to the DMCA limitations on liability. Ironically released the same day as the Federal Trade Commission's initiative to *protect* personal online privacy, it is hard to imagine how PPI's proposal for *less* consumer privacy could be acceptable.

Second, hundreds of small Internet companies are offering services to consumers free of charge, in return for minimal anonymous or unverified demographic information. The PPI proposal may unintentionally thwart these emerging beneficial consumer services by giving the Internet businesses a Hobson's choice: either they could try to collect and verify personal information, which could drastically reduce consumer acceptance of these new business models; or, they could forego qualification for the DMCA limitations of liability, which could hinder their ability to obtain financing.

Finally, tying the collection and monitoring of personal behavior to copyright liability sets a highly dangerous precedent. In the future, when all consumer playback and recording devices are connected across home digital networks that are online to the Internet, the temptation surely will exist to monitor all consumer activity to ferret out acts of infringement. In enacting the DMCA, Congress specifically rejected attempts to impose intrusive obligations on service providers, and refused to deputize service and technology companies as the "Internet police." PPI asks Congress to recalibrate the DMCA so as to reverse this course -- effectively, to strike the first match on the theory that the resulting intrusions will begin a controlled burn and not a firestorm. HRRC respectfully believes that the potential for conflagration is not worth the candle.

Conclusion

The HRRC applauds the Committee's interest in understanding the needs of small businesses on the Internet. We urge the Committee and Congress not to precipitously alter existing legal principles that have well-served both copyright and public interests over the past decades, and to move cautiously in revisiting carefully crafted compromises reached only recently in the DMCA.

Respectfully submitted,

Ruth Rodgers
Executive Director

4

HRRC CORE PRINCIPLES

1. *Fair Use remains vital to consumer welfare in the digital age. Consumers should continue to be able to engage in time-shifting, place-shifting, and other private, noncommercial rendering of lawfully obtained music and video content.*

   ♦ Application of any technical measures should recognize fair use principles through "recording" rule limitations.

   ♦ Consumer fair use rendering of content may include consumer-to-consumer exchanges.

2. *Products and services with substantial non-infringing uses, including those that enable fair use activities by consumers, should continue to be legal.*

   ♦ The Supreme Court's holding in the "Betamax" case has been essential for new and beneficial technology, products, and services to reach consumers.

3. *Home recording practices have nothing to do with commercial retransmission of signals, unauthorized commercial reproduction of content, or other acts of "piracy." Home recording and piracy should not be confused.*

   ♦ Such unlawful commercial activity occurs whether or not consumers have access to home recording technology, so ordinary consumers need not and should not be the target of efforts to deter it.

4. *Any technical constraints imposed on products or consumers by law, license or regulation should be narrowly tailored and construed, should not hinder technological innovation, and may be justified only to the extent that they foster the availability of content to consumers.*

   ♦ Application of a technical measure that would entirely prevent a consumer from making audio home recordings on devices or media covered by the Audio Home Recording Act should be considered illegal under the Act.

   ♦ The Digital Millennium Copyright Act should not be construed so as to mandate design conformance of a consumer electronics product or a computing product with any particular technical measure (other than the narrow, limited exception specified in section 1201(k) of the Act).

   ♦ The Federal Communications Commission should not permit cable entities or others to deny lawful viewing of DTV signals to consumers based on copy protection concerns over product interfaces.

Testimony of

The Future of Music Coalition

on

Online Music: Will Small Music Labels and Entrepreneurs Prosper in the Internet Age?

Before the

House Small Business Committee

United States House of Representatives

May, 24 2000

contact: Jennifer Toomey, simplejt@aol.com, 202 518-4117
                 Michael Bracy, mbracy@bracywilliams.com, 202 661-2065

Future of Music Coalition
601 13th Street, N.W.
Suite 900 South
Washington, DC 20005
Phone 202.783.5588
FAX 202.783 5595
www.futureofmusic.com

Introduction

The Future of Music Coalition is a collaboration between leading independent musicians and experts from the worlds of technology, public policy and copyright law. The primary mission of the organization is to create an environment for artists who do not fear technology to work with technology professionals who have the best interests of artists at heart. This collaboration will lead to greater understanding from both sides, and ideally move toward solutions to issues that possibly threaten the traditional revenue streams of independent artists.

There is a general misconception that a single music "industry" exists – rather, there are multiple industries that have coexisted for decades. The major labels are multinational corporations that dominate radio play and album sales. The independent (indie) music industry, on the other hand, is responsible for an overwhelming majority of music released into the marketplace. While the independent industry is a stepping stone for some who hope to achieve stardom through the major labels, for many artists working independently is their way of maintaining control both over their finances and their art.

It is our belief that indie artists will be disproportionately affected by a loss of revenue in a post-copyright era. Future of Music is issuing a challenge to all those working in the Internet music business to put their "substitute royalties" and ancillary revenue streams where their music-fan mouths are and to figure out a legitimate way to compensate musicians for their songs. We are excited to support any innovative payment strategy that seems feasible, and we refuse to support any business model that does not guard the financial value of musicians' labor.

It's the end of copyright era! Or so you would think if you had been listening to the majority position at Internet music conferences. What does that mean for the artists and musicians who stand to lose mechanical royalties as a revenue source? Nothing good.

Royalties 101

For the past 50 years, most musicians have been compensated through a variety of revenue-generating activities: selling CDs, playing shows, radio play, or licensing their songs to TV or movies. Almost all of this money falls under three umbrellas -- mechanical royalties, artist royalties and performance royalties.

In order to understand the difference between these three types of royalties, it's important to understand that there are two different claims of copyright on every piece of recorded music. One focuses on the "sound recording" and one focuses on the "underlying work" or, in other words, the intangible intellectual property that is a "song."

2

91

Mechanical royalties are paid to the songwriter per unit sold. Artist royalties are paid to the performer of the song per unit sold. Performance royalties are paid to the performer and the songwriter when the song is broadcast (TV, Radio, Jukebox, etc). Physical CD sales generate artist royalties, which are split between the label and the band/artist.

Even in this nutshell explanation of royalties you can get a sense of how complicated this payment system can be. We are not discussing the standard royalty breakdown at major labels in this testimony, but there are several books that explain the subject in detail, including Donald Passman's book All You Need to Know about the Music Industry.

In our experience in the independent music community, many labels and bands simplify the payment system by agreeing to a profit split, where the net profits from sales are usually split 50/50 after the costs of manufacturing and promotion are covered. With a profit split it's understood that the mechanicals and artists royalties are folded into one payment, since the songwriter and performer are usually the same person. For example, if the independent label Simple Machines sells 5000 CDs by the band Ida to the distributor for $6, which in turn sells them to stores, that's $30,000 in gross profit. If each CD costs about $2.00 to make, that's about $10,000 in costs. Doing the math: $30,000 gross - $10,000 costs = $20,000 net profit. Split 50/50 it's $10,000 for the label and $10,000 for the band. This example is based on 5000 CDs....imagine the potential profits if you're a band like Sleater-Kinney that's selling 20,000+. Of course, they have more expenses but, all in all, it's clear from this example and from our experience that mechanical royalties are the most significant source of revenue for independent bands and artists.

Basic royalties also generate a huge chunk of revenue for major label bands. Artists who control the copyright in the underlying song are guaranteed basic royalties on every unit sold under the Copyright Statute, whether the album has broken even or not. Considering how much the deck is stacked against major label artists, this is sometimes the only guaranteed source of revenue, aside from any advances. (Major label artists are forced to play by accounting practices muddled with crazy caveats, advances and "points" that we can't tackle in this testimony.)

Why It's The End

The fundamental way that this mechanical royalty system has worked over the years is that the record labels had access to the three components needed to mass produce the music: the master tapes, the means of production, and the distribution channels. With the recent advances in digital technology, labels are losing their exclusive control over all three. Digital technology allows for perfect copies, so every store-bought CD becomes, in essence, a master tape. Plus, the cost of buying the means of production -- CD burners -- has dropped into a widely affordable price range. And now, because of digital download technology, the distribution of music itself is changing.

Now we're faced with a huge problem: piracy. As eloquently stated by Brian Zisk: "If music can be heard, it can be copied." In the same way that cassette recorders enabled low-fi pirates (or high-school nerds) to illegally record Doobie Brothers concerts or stow away illegal copies of Casey Casum's Top Twenty countdowns (albeit with poor quality), MP3s and digital download technology are making it simple to copy and send near-perfect quality music files across the Internet.

Music Business Fights Back

This is what all the record labels are talking about when they are pointing fingers and yelling "bloody piracy!" What are they gonna do about it? Their solution is two-fold:

1. Fiercely enforce the existing copyright laws through the courts and government.

2. Find a way to encrypt music files in order to make it impossible to copy or send files illegally.

But how does it work? Unless you're the kind of masochist who longs for the comfort of Big Brother and a world where our computers are legally policed for our own good and the good of the community, you can already see the impending problems with chasing down Internet piracy. As for solution number two, from what I've been told, it's impossible to come up with an encryption program that is crack proof. The basic explanation of that position says that any encryption program is just a mathematical algorithm. If it can be written, it can be unwritten -- it's just a scientific fact. I don't know if this is true (I can't even spell "algorithm" much less "unwrite" one) but for the most part the smartest, hippest computer folks that we speak with are all in agreement on this point. Plus, the anecdotal evidence speaks volumes. DVD code has been hacked to work on Linux machines, and Microsoft's supposedly "impervious" music encryption program was hacked within a day of its launch.

True or not, it's fair to say things have changed and it's going to be quite difficult getting the copyright genie back in its seemingly broken bottle. It is very likely that musicians are facing a future where it will be impossible for labels to ever fully secure music files to prohibit piracy and to ensure that those who create music are compensated.

Benefits of Digital Downloads

What does that mean for the artists? That depends on who you ask. For the most part, music fans that work in the Internet community believe that the overwhelming benefits of digital download technology outweigh impending copyright failures. Their argument is based on a belief that digital download technology frees artists from the stranglehold of major label, media and chain store monopolies.

Before the Internet age, artists had to sign over the majority of their potential profits and align themselves with corporations in order to attain a certain level of national distribution or radio airplay. Now with the Internet, musicians can download free software to encode their songs as MP3s and sell near-perfect quality music directly to anyone who comes to their website. Gone are the days when manufacturing, distribution, shipping and storage costs made it impossible for indie artists and labels to compete with major distribution sources. With digital downloads there are minimal manufacturing and distribution costs and, theoretically, immediate access to an international audience.

Post-CD World

Sounds great, doesn't it? Even better news is the fact that, at least for now, MP3s seem to be increasing CD sales rather than reducing them. Anecdotal evidence suggests that bands that are most pirated will also see a general increase in CD sales. The obvious parallel here is radio, where free access to a band's single often drives sales for the album. But this is what's happening now when CDs are still the preferred format for music consumption. What happens if CDs as a format become less relevant?

Many of the very same music fans that work in the Internet and love talking about the wonderful "post copyright" age are also, ironically, creating business models based on the belief that a majority of music sales will eventually go entirely digital. If digital distribution becomes the preferred method for music consumption and there is no foolproof way to encrypt downloaded songs, then it's fair to say that a whole lot of artists who would have made money selling CDs will lose those future potential digital sales to piracy.

Leaving Mechanicals Out of the Internet Business Model

So what are these entrepreneurial music fans doing to ensure that the artists they love will get paid for their music? Not very much, as far as we can tell. There seems to be a basic lack of understanding displayed by many of these Internet companies about how artists actually make the lion's share of their money now. Without the slightest twinge of irony, panelist after panelist would cheer the end of antiquated copyright protection while holding up a nebulous new carrot for the artist to pursue: Ancillary Revenue Streams.

A Plate of Paprika

Ancillary Revenue Streams (ARS) are just what they sound like: other ways to make money off of music. Some examples of ARS are touring, or selling

5

songs to movies and television. These streams are not new. Artists have always supplemented their royalties by playing live and selling music through other channels but, up to now, those means of getting paid were always seen as spice on the meat and potatoes of mechanical royalties. To hear these Internet tech heads speak you'd think that as musicians in the Internet age we're going to be expected to live on a plate of paprika.

Here are just some of the most obvious problems with ARS as a substitute for mechanical royalties within the independent music community.

1. Touring

While touring is a great way for bands to raise their profile, make fans and generate press, it is very rarely a big money maker in its own right. For the most part, only the most successful smaller scale indie acts and the huge major label acts make money on tour. Ironically, major label acts often make the majority of their tour profit because of ancillary to ancillary streams in the form of corporate tour sponsorships.

For example, Lauryn Hill's tour last summer was sponsored by Levi's. Because of these sponsorships, bands are able to defray the massive costs of going on tour, which often includes a hefty road crew, semi-trucks, staging, buses, hotels and paying the traveling musicians. Without sponsorships, many hugely successful artists would never break even on the road. Even an internationally-acclaimed and Grammy winning artist like Beck who refused sponsorship contracts generally lost money on sellout tours and had to eat those tour support losses out of his major label royalties (these are the same royalties that would disappear in a post-copyright world). While the Internet might make an artist free of major labels through the benefits of digital downloads, it will very likely make them prisoners to sponsorship deals with other corporations.

Well-known indie bands like Fugazi and Superchunk can make money touring but that is often due to their streamlined operations, meticulous attention to booking details, and willingness to sleep on floors. Even with the frugality, margins on these bands' tour revenues are generally quite tight. It's not unusual to hear stories of how the majority of a tour's profits disappeared the moment the band's van broke down.

Profits also disappear if a band raises the stakes i.e. if they choose to tour with their own PA or light set up, or through larger clubs that involve more expensive advertising campaigns, more security, and union-scale pay.

Furthermore, it's often difficult for bands to write good music or live fulfilling lives if they have to pull up the stakes every few months just to ensure they can meet their mortgage payments. And we all know what's going to happen when these artists decide they'd like to have a family. If there are no mechanical royalties and touring is a musician's primary means of support, it's not difficult to guess that these rockers will hang up the ax and get a day job. Rolling Stones aside, we all understand that the overwhelming majority of musicians will not be touring into their 30's and 40's. This just continues to ensure that the majority of music will be made by teenagers for teenagers.

2. Music for TV Commercials Movies
It's good work...if you can get it. The most common route from rock record to TV commercial is through a publishing company. If you know how that works you can skip ahead. If not, here's the summary:

Performance Rights Associations:
When a songwriter writes a song s/he is the sole owner of that copyright. If that artist wants to receive royalties from radio play, TV or movie soundtracks, he or she has to align with one of the two non-profit performance rights associations, ASCAP or BMI, or with the one for-profit organization, SESAC. These associations take a percentage of the artist's royalty as payment for their "work" collecting royalties from radio stations and other places where the artist's work is publicly performed.

The payment system is based on a complicated formula that weights potential audience, time of day and song duration in order to come up with a "per play" rate. An artist whose song gets played at Superbowl halftime will make a lot more money than a song that's played on the local rock station in Des Moines at 3 am. Performance royalties generated by radio play can be a significant source of money for artists, but only if you're part of the commercial radio world. We're sure that Led Zeppelin is getting some serious cash from BMI or ASCAP every three months, but what about the throngs of bands that don't get radio play? Tsunami is registered with BMI, and our average quarterly royalty check is, oh, about $30. The bottom line is there is no other way to participate in this revenue stream without aligning with the performing rights organizations -- BMI, ASCAP or SESAC. Furthermore, what are the chances that your work will be played consistently on radio stations that have a significant audience share? Unless you're being pushed by a major label radio promoter, they're next to nothing.

Publishing Companies:
Next in line for a bite of your performance royalties are the publishing companies. There are many different types of deals but these groups generally take a half of your total royalties (i.e. mechanicals, performance, synchronization, etc.) as payment for trying to get more of your songs used in TV shows, commercials and movies. The theory is this: a well known publishing company with friends in high places is more likely to be in a position to get your song in the new Coke commercial than you would

7

be while you are sitting in your garage rocking out with your buddies. You know you can make a lot more money from a Coke commercial than you can playing in the local bar, so you make the decision to risk another half of your potential performance royalties in order to benefit from the publishing company's connections.

Royalties for Film/TV/Ad Placements:
When a song is licensed for film, TV or ad placements there is a synchronization license and associated royalties for the use of the song, as well as a master use license and any associated royalties for the use for the recording. The sync royalties are paid to the songwriter and publisher, and the master use royalties will go to the record company and the artist. These are generally negotiable fees set on a one time basis to cover whatever uses are intended.

Getting Paid
Now that we understand the basic mechanics of performance royalties and publishing, let's apply this to ARS and consider how this kind of TV and movie work will take up the slack for mechanical royalties that will disappear in the "post copyright age". For starters let's take a second and think about how many of your friends have had songs in motion pictures and on television. Good, now think about how many of them get steady work like that. Great, now think about how many of them are actually getting paid the full amount of what they are legally due for a royalty in that situation.

Getting Paid Less
Oh yeah, we forgot to mention that, although there are standards and protections, it's not uncommon that artist get paid less than they're worth. Despite its flaws, copyright law has attempted to protect the rights of the songwriter in the face of the monopoly (big capital). Thanks to copyright law and music unions, certain rates were put in place to guarantee players a certain wage, per hour, per song, per play, etc. This was a way to use the collective bargaining power of writers to guarantee they didn't get bowled over by corporate power.

Major labels, TV networks and movie companies realized they had an easy way to get around that. They would do the same thing that the publishing companies did. They would say to the artist, "Hey, we'd really like to use your song for our show, but we don't want to have to pay you the full amount of money that the law says we should pay you, including residual royalties for reruns etc. So how about you sign away your rights to residual royalties and we'll give you this prestigious position on our TV show and a chunk of money?"

Most artists in this position say, "Well, that's a lot of money and if they don't use my song they will use someone else's so I guess I will let the TV show pay me less than I deserve to get."

The Mechanism for Underpayment

There you have it, ladies and gentlemen, the mechanism for underpaying artists that exists in every area of the major music business. Did you know, for example, that MTV's basic video submission agreement states that if you give them a tape for possible play you agree to allow them to use the music for incidental footage at a reduced royalty rate. This means that if you ever hope to have MTV play your video on 120 Minutes you have to agree to give them the rights to let them use your music elsewhere at a reduced rate.

These trade-offs are so common that even respected musicians will agree to get paid less than they deserve. For example, Alex Chilton whose Big Star anthem "In The Street" graces the opening moments of "That '70s Show" has been quoted saying that he is taking home an alleged chicken scratch of $70 each time a new show airs. Compare that with the amount of revenue that same station charges for 30 seconds of commercial time and you'll understand how inadequate this ancillary revenue stream is as a replacement for mechanical royalties.

What's worse, this new post-copyright world where music is "free" just serves to reinforce the clearly demonstrated desire of business interests to avoid having to pay fair wages to musicians for their work. "After all, if no one else is paying for music why should the corporations have to?"

3. Merchandise sales

Some bands make a lot of money on merchandise, some make less. There are several problems with this as a substitute for mechanical royalties. First of all, it's not a steady stream of income. To sell a t-shirt, you most likely have to be on tour, and as noted in item 1, sometimes that's a losing proposition in itself. In some cases, bands sell merchandise because it's the ONLY way they can make money on tour. But the bigger problem with depending on t-shirt sales as a new revenue stream is the very nature of the argument. Bands write songs and play music, so they should be compensated for their skills as musicians, not for their skills in making a neat sticker or beer cozy.

4. Websites and Ad Revenue from "Click Throughs"

Now this is an interesting one. Some of the genius internet panelists are suggesting that artists should set up a subscription area of their websites where they ask folks to pay a certain amount of money to get into that private area because they are your fans. The same argument that was made about the difficulties in encrypting music applies here. If it's impossible for Microsoft to create a method of encrypting music then how do indie rocker novices insure that only the proper people get into our restricted sites?

Another idea that has been implemented on a number of MP3-based sites is sharing advertising revenue with artists. On these mega-MP3 sites, the name of the game is traffic. The number of unique visitors to the site is held up to investors and potential advertisers as a powerful indicator of the site's popularity and influence. But it's rough going out there -- nowadays bands and artists have lots of choices as to where they post their sound files. In order to entice more bands and artists, some sites have started to reward bands that direct fans (aka "eyeballs") to that site by giving them a cut of advertising revenue. Others have taken it one step further and rewarded bands for "click through" traffic that comes to their site based on band-generated links. Considering that these free MP3-based sites have paid virtually nothing for the content that has, in turn, propelled these companies to multi-million dollar IPOs, sharing a bit of the ad revenue seems like the right thing to do. Still, this is not a legitimate ancillary revenue stream. From what we hear, revenue sharing programs pay artists a pittance. Who knows, this model might turn into an interesting way to supplement artists' revenues, but as it stands, it's not successful. Indie artists should not be expected to give up actual payment for hypothetical payment.

Even more, these models further reduce the artist's role to a pawn in a much larger chess game. Sure, we all participate in the capitalist system, but this kind of stream has nothing to do with the intrinsic value of the artist's work. The idea behind mechanical royalties is that music is valuable and that the workers who create this music should be compensated for that music. I find it humiliating that these internet companies see nothing wrong in unseating the value of my work (work that their business models benefit from) and then giving me the responsibility of getting paid for some unproved ancillary sizzle.

5. Virtual Tip Jars
This theory proposes that artists set up an area on their site where fans can volunteer to pay them money. Ha ha ha! We're not musicians, we're trained monkeys! Actually, there is precedent for this business model in open-source software development where users are asked to pay an honorary donation for the privilege of using a software program. The difference here, however, is that open source software developers have the choice to give away their work, whereas in the post-copyright era where music is seen as free, artists may not have that choice

6. Grants and Foundations
This is the theory that instead of paying musicians for their work, we can turn to government or to privately endowed foundations to support the arts like they do in Europe and Canada. It would be wonderful to be able to put out

our own records, like Canada's Julie Doiron did this year. It would be even nicer to be able to apply for and receive government touring grants, as she has done. Even better, she was not only eligible but capable of winning the Juno award (Canada's Grammy). Still, after 32 years of life in this bastion of capitalism I don't see that transformation happening here any time soon.

What's worse, without a cultural history that respects this kind of patronage we would be setting our labor up as somehow less valuable than other general types of labor that are paid through the market. It's easy to see how artists would become second class citizens in this scenario, not workers, with a valuable contribution that deserves to be compensated but arbitrarily endowed artisans looking for charity. Oh, and we all know that artists are never influenced by their patrons. That's why many bands stop taking risks once they're aligned with a major label.

Is ARS All Bad?

Don't get us wrong, there are people who make a majority of their money through ancillary streams. Actually, many of the most outspoken musicians who are supporting Internet music commerce these days are setting themselves up to make a bundle through other channels. Chuck D himself has said that he will use his music as a loss leader in order to raise money in other areas. If his website rapstation.com becomes the main portal for rap information on the Internet, he won't need to worry much about Public Enemy mechanicals -- he can make his cash selling ads or mailing lists. The same is true for Thomas Dolby <http://www.beatnik.com> and his internet music software and Jerry Harrison from the Talking Heads and his garageband.com site. These folks saw the changes coming down the pipe and they got into the fray. We don't fault them for it one bit; they are doing the smart thing and adapting to a changing world. They are working hard and they should be compensated. What worries us is that these articulate artists get paraded around as spokepersons for the artist in the post copyright age when they've all got their personal houses in order. How many rapstation.coms can there be out there? Will all rappers benefit equally from the post copyright age? Hardly.

Worse for the Indies?

No, it doesn't look too good for musicians in a post copyright age, and it looks the worst for those who have been working in the indie communities with no thought of working with the majors. Think about it; indie artists have already disassociated from the traditional promotion and distribution chains, albeit on a smaller, more expensive level by relying on mailorder and mom and pop stores. This Internet technology offers better distribution and a higher profile at a cheaper price, but many indie artists were never much tied to the shackles of the corporate ogre in the first place, so those gains are somewhat moot.

What's worse, every sale indie artists lose comes out of their own pockets. This is doubly distressing considering the fact that many who work in indies are

100

also musicians who have never relied on these traditional ancillary revenue streams in the first place. Furthermore, when you realize that the great majority of people who are trafficking in pirated digital downloads are college students (the demographic that makes up great majority of the indie buyers) it just follows basic logic to believe that indies are being disproportionately affected.

Now What?

What should indie artists do? It's hard to say. The RIAA is clearly identified with the interests of the major labels and therefore more considered by many to be more worthy of contempt than support. On the other hand the great majority of the entrepreneurial Internet music folks who are developing these new technologies and services often really do seem to care about musicians. Their belief in open-source technology which informs their rationale for moving towards "free music" is utopian and idealistic so they are an interesting group to align with, aside from the fact that their technological innovations erase the value of artists' music production. Maybe I'm giving them the benefit of the doubt, but it just seems that they have had other things on their mind besides guarding our rights.

The Challenge To Do Better

The Future of Music Coalition repeats the challenge it issued to those working in Internet music business community to put their substitute royalties where their music-fan mouths are and to figure out a legitimate way to compensate musicians for their work. We are excited to support any payment strategy that seems feasible, and we refuse to support any business model that does not guard the financial value of our labor. Gone are the days when Internet companies can say they are working to compensate the artist without really doing so.

Second, we issued a challenge to all the innovative members of the Internet community to create legitimate business models that will not only utilize the power of the Internet, but fairly compensate artists for their work.

Third, we challenged all the musicians, artists and members of the independent music community to think hard about their position on these issues before they choose to participate in systems that may end up being a bust or boon.

We applaud you again for holding this important hearing and taking an interest in issues of importance to the Independent music community.